AUG 0 3 2010

FOSTERING COMMUNITY THROUGH DIGITAL STORYTELLING

A Guide for Academic Libraries

Anne M. Fields and Karen R. Diaz

A Member of the Greenwood Publishing Group

Westport, Connecticut • London

Library of Congress Cataloging-in-Publication Data

Fields, Anne M.
Fostering community through digital storytelling : a guide for academic
libraries / Anne M. Fields and Karen R. Diaz.
   p.   cm.
   Includes bibliographical references and index.
   ISBN 978–1–59158–552–7 (alk. paper)
   1. Academic libraries—Public relations.   2. Digital storytelling.   3. Libraries
and colleges.   4. Communication in organizations.   I. Díaz, Karen R.   II. Title.
   Z716.3.F54   2008
   027.62'51—dc22   2007049024

British Library Cataloguing in Publication Data is available.

Copyright © 2008 by Libraries Unlimited

All rights reserved. No portion of this book may be
reproduced, by any process or technique, without the
express written consent of the publisher.

Library of Congress Catalog Card Number: 2007049024
ISBN: 978–1–59158–552–7

First published in 2008

Libraries Unlimited, 88 Post Road West, Westport, CT 06881
A Member of the Greenwood Publishing Group, Inc.
www.lu.com

Printed in the United States of America

The paper used in this book complies with the
Permanent Paper Standard issued by the National
Information Standards Organization (Z39.48–1984).

10 9 8 7 6 5 4 3 2 1

Contents

Preface

This is the story of why we decided to write this book.

In April 2005, we first heard about digital storytelling while investigating new learning trends in higher education as part of a task force on libraries and learning. At the same time, one of our assistant directors—attracted by content displayed on digital billboards outside the Shanghai University Library—was also learning about digital storytelling from his Chinese hosts. When he returned from China he offered us the opportunity to attend a digital storytelling workshop in Asheville, North Carolina, led by Joe Lambert of the Center for Digital Storytelling. Intrigued, we set off on our journey to Asheville.

The Center for Digital Storytelling's intensive three-day workshops allow participants to work on stories individually or with a partner. We decided to work together and so needed to pick an experience we had in common. Anticipating the major library renovation that Ohio State University would be undertaking beginning in 2006, we chose to do a story about work we had done together on a library renovation committee. We wrote and rewrote, we gathered pictures, we recorded different voices reading parts of our script, we gathered music, and we headed off to the workshop, quite pleased with how organized we were.

The first thing we learned about digital storytelling was the social process involved. Even if you come with a story already written, the first step in the workshop is to engage in a story circle in which you share your story with the group. In our story circle we heard stories of adoption, love, family relationships, identity crises, and more. Our story, based on committee work and the last to be shared, seemed embarrassingly dull. But we bravely shared it, and we benefited, as did everyone, from the group's reactions. Two things happened. First, we realized the story needed to be our own story, the story of Anne and Karen, not the story of the Ohio State University Libraries. And second, we learned that *everyone* has a library story to tell–at least one. The story circle transformed both our story and our outlook on storytelling.

The next big thing we learned about digital storytelling was that this could be a transformational way of talking not only about ourselves but also about libraries. The first-person nature of a digital story draws the listener into caring about what the storyteller has to say. In this age of the invisible library of digitized collections and services, digital storytelling can make the people who work in libraries visible again.

The final big lesson of digital storytelling is a lesson we are still learning, and that we hope to share with you. It is the lesson of how transformational digital storytelling can be not only in telling the library's story, but also in discovering the library's story. Digital storytelling allows us to talk to each other reflectively and to engage our users in conversation about libraries. It allows us to think about library transformation with the right side of the brain.

Reaching in and finding our creative side is challenging but exhilarating. Moving from creating a single story to creating a whole program of digital storytelling in a library or on an entire campus is even more challenging but equally exhilarating. We have begun this journey, and our experience informs this book. Writing this book informs our journey.

Acknowledgments

We would like to thank Libraries Unlimited for permission to reuse portions of our chapter "Digital Storytelling, Libraries, and Community" published in *Library 2.0 and Beyond: Innovative Technologies and Tomorrow's User*, Nancy Courtney (Ed.). We also would like to thank Joe Lambert and the Center for Digital Storytelling. Their vision of the power of digital storytelling will always inspire our work.

Introduction

We are all aware of how the academic library landscape is changing. Online Computer Library Center (OCLC) provides us with annual environmental scans and other reports that examine where technology is heading and if and where libraries are fitting into those changing environments. We often hear talk of "crises" in academic libraries: scholarly communication, diminishing reference statistics, the Googlization of information access, for example. In the *2003 OCLC Environmental Scan: Pattern Recognition*, De Rosa, Dempsey, and Wilson (2004, 2) comment on the defensive, even "testy" response of the library community to these challenges: "Why don't 'they' get it that libraries and librarians are useful, relevant and important in the age of Google?" We are left devising strategies to counteract these trends and to reinsert ourselves into the mainstream of university and student life, relying in a more or less left-brained way on data, studies, logic, and our own academic training. To talk about these concerns otherwise looks like self-serving and unseemly whining. And yet if we do not act, we fear not only our own irrelevance but worse, a diminishment of the intellectual rigor involved in the information process and a loss of concern for the common good that libraries have always played in this process.

This book proposes digital storytelling as a more creative, right-brained way of talking about the library's present condition and future directions to help others understand us and to help us understand ourselves. Digital stories are brief multimodal digital videos that, in the case of the academic library, engage libraries in personal conversations with their communities. Unlike traditional academic discourse, digital stories embrace the emotional side of experience in order to engage listeners. After all, everyone loves a good story.

People tell stories, and people listen to stories, for many reasons. Individuals tell stories in order to organize and make sense of their experiences in an increasingly confusing world. They tell stories in order to remember. Cultures—be they universities, corporations, religions ethnic groups, or nations—tell stories to shape and maintain their histories and identities. These stories help people communicate experiences with one another and through that communication to build community. People listen to stories because they love the humor, the pathos, and the engagement of being present in the moment of the storyteller's lived experience.

Digital story may be differently defined depending on the context in which it is being used. For example, in a K-12 environment creating a digital story may involve recasting an already told story into a PowerPoint presentation using student art and voiceover narration. Businesses have been using digital stories since the early 1980s to convey to their employees company histories, traditions, and values. More recently, some companies have been incorporating the first-person nature of digital storytelling into their advertising. For our purposes we define digital story as a three- to five-minute video that uses some combination of still images, video clips, music, and the writer's own voiceover narration to convey a dramatic point from the writer's own point of view. Perhaps more important than the story, however, is the process of the creation of that story. Through the workshopping of the story script in what is called a "story circle," storytellers often find themselves transformed in sometimes subtle, sometimes profound ways. Those who help storytellers craft their stories receive similar benefits.

The new twenty-first-century social technologies that are an everyday part of today's college student's life have defined new social contexts to which academic libraries must pay attention if they want to survive. *YouTube*, social bookmarking, *iTunesU*, podcasting, vlogcasting, gaming, and *MySpace* and *Facebook* are only a few of the technological phenomena that allow people to be alone but together at the same time. In this new environment the digital storytelling movement planted by Dana Atchley and Joe Lambert at the Center for Digital Storytelling in Berkeley, California, has emerged to allow people to connect socially within and beyond their communities. The *I-10 Witness Project*, National Public Radio's *StoryCorps* and the British Broadcasting Corporation's *Capture Wales Project* all represent movements to collect stories, some with video, some with music, but all with the narrators telling their own stories in their own voices.

Our academic library users, as well as the students who do not use our libraries, come to the university as products of this new technologically driven social climate. They also bring with them new preferences for learning that are influencing the ways in which teaching is conducted at the university level. Students prefer active and collaborative learning. They are becoming much more involved as undergraduates in original research, and—when allowed—are opting to display their learning through such multimodal products as electronic portfolios, videos, and podcasts, rather than or in addition to text-based research papers and examinations. Students can use digital stories as a means of reflecting on their learning and also as a multimodal evidence of their learning. Such learning places much more responsibility on the learner, however, which in turn requires careful scaffolding of learning by the instructor. Faculty can use digital stories in a variety of ways to enhance their teaching. They can use them to pose questions, to engage students in a controversial question, and to bring subject concepts to life. By telling stories of their own research they can humanize themselves to their students.

What role can digital storytelling play in the academic library, especially in this era of Googlization, scholarly communication crises, increasingly virtual access to collections and services and the resulting alleged decrease in the need for library as place? Unique among campus units, the academic library not only supports the teaching, learning and research needs of faculty and students but it is a teaching unit in and of itself. Libraries then are almost small corporations and can use digital stories for internal organizational development. Stories can be an important tool for marketing library collections and services, and they can play a role in fund-raising by bringing to life the impact that libraries can have on the lives of students and faculty. At their very heart, however, libraries are teaching and learning units that resemble academic departments. Just as a faculty member in sociology might tell a story of Somali refugee family surviving in a U.S. urban environment, the library can use digital storytelling to tell the story of a rare manuscript, its author, and even the donor whose love of letters brought the collection to the library.

How does an academic library build a program of digital storytelling within the library and then extend it to the wider campus? It can start with a single intensive three-day workshop for a small group of library staff and nonlibrary faculty. It develops with the help of partners from around the campus. Together we share mutual challenges, including human subjects rules, the blurriness of copyright law, file storage, competition for funding, training needs, differing agendas, and even territoriality.

Together, though, we also have unique gifts to share: content, expertise, institutional repositories, and technology. The library's particular gifts include metadata creation, provision of primary content for stories, and the ability to locate, negotiate, and make available copyright-free images and music. Ultimately, the library cannot create a rich program of digital storytelling for itself without collaborating with campus partners. The library particularly needs to find curricular partners, that is, faculty who will embed libraries and librarians in their courses and in their research in order to allow us to gather the stories of student learning and faculty research that result from their use of our collections and services.

This book will examine the potential role of stories within the academic library. It also will examine the potential value to librarians, staff, student assistants, as well as nonlibrary faculty and students, of the very act of telling those stories. Libraries create digital stories to grow our organizations; to reach out to and to listen to our users; to enhance interdisciplinary activities; and to create the new campus collaborations that will foster a deeper and richer campus community. Libraries are moving from the metaphor of "heart of the university" to a new metaphor of "crossroads of the community." While data, studies, and logic can help map that path, only stories can help us build community while on that path.

REFERENCES

British Broadcasting Corporation. (June 12, 2007). *Capture Wales Project.* Retrieved June 12, 2007, from http://www.bbc.co.uk/wales/capturewales.

DeRosa, Cathy, Lorcan Dempsey, and Alane Wilson. (2004). *The 2003 OCLC environmental scan: Pattern recognition: A report to the OCLC membership.* Dublin, OH: OCLC.

I-10 Witness Project. (n.d.). Retrieved June 12, 2007, from http://i10witness.org/.

iTunesU. (n.d.). Retrieved June 12, 2007, from http://www.apple.com/education/itunesu/.

National Public Radio. (n.d.). *StoryCorps.* Retrieved June 12, 2007, from http://www.storycorps.net/.

CHAPTER 1
What Are Stories, and Why Do We Tell Them?

DEFINING STORY

The *Oxford English Dictionary* (2007) offers many dry definitions of the word *story*; for instance: "The series of events in the life of a person or the past existence of a thing, country, institution, etc., considered as narrated or as a subject for narration," and, "An incident, real or fictitious, related in conversation or in written discourse in order to amuse or interest, or to illustrate some remark made; an anecdote." Children, however, do not need a definition. They know what stories are and what story means almost intuitively. In fact, even three-year-olds are capable of telling stories for a number of reasons ranging from simply telling what has gone on in their lives on a particular day to telling a story that will help them accomplish a purpose (Stein and Kissel 2005): "Grandpa took us to the zoo today, Mommy. We saw a real tiger." "Ben took my cookie. I think he needs a time-out."

As their lives become more complicated, and their cognitive and language abilities better developed, so do the stories. The story about the trip to the zoo grows from a simple tale of "Grandpa took us to the zoo, and we saw a real tiger" to "My grandpa took my cousins and me to the zoo because they were visiting from Illinois and we always do fun things like that together. The best thing I saw was the tiger. He was bigger than any animal I've ever seen. He paced and paced and paced around his cage. I think he was interested in me. I'd like to work in a zoo someday, especially with the tigers." The child begins to insert bits of family history ("We always do fun things together"), to project himself into the tiger's mind ("I think he was interested in me"), and even to look into the future ("I'd like to work in a zoo someday"). Still, the child does not worry about how to define stories; he just tells them.

The word *story* becomes much more parsed as academe lays claim to it, distinguishing (sometimes) *story* from *narrative, narrative* from *narration*, and *narration* from *plot* or *discourse*, but certainly not consistently so, as they separate what happened from how those happenings are shaped into a discourse of some kind. Surrounded by all this arguing over what many nonacademics sometimes characterize as semantics, story sometimes has taken on the reputation of being something less than narrative. Hauerwas believes that this may be due to the fact that story is often considered something less than the truth or reality because truth or reality is difficult, perhaps impossible, to discern or articulate: "Thus, when we are children we make do with stories, but when we grow up we want the literal truth—that is, the truth that can be substantiated apart from the story . . . Stories create a fantasy world that releases us from the burden of having to deal with the real world" (Hauerwas 1983, 25). This bifurcation of story from truth, agrees McEwan (1995), also is a sign of a modern need for scientific objectivity. Using the words *story* and *narrative* synonymously, Kreiswirth sees that "story gets blamed for the behavior of its evil twin, fable. On this view, whatever else it is, narrative, by its very form as narrative, is false, a fiction, something 'imposed' on pre- or non-narrative phenomena [and] . . . always potentially a tall tale" (Kreiswirth 2000, 312). He carefully points out, however, that "a true story, one that claims to represent actual happenings . . . works as a communicative act exactly the same way as a fictional story, one that doesn't make such claims . . . Narrative still functions as narrative—as a means of apprehending, depicting, and/or communicating temporal and causal relationships between agents and events—regardless of what use it is being put to" (Kreiswirth 2000, 313).

Ironically, we have experienced something of a minor power struggle over what to call the subject of this book on our own campus, digital *stories* or digital *narratives*, digital narratives being thought by some to have broader appeal within an institution known internationally for its study of narrative. We hold fast to the term digital *stories* for this book. First, the noun *stories* can be transformed easily into the verbal noun *storytelling*. We believe that the act and process of the telling is as important as the final product, as we will discuss in subsequent chapters. *Narrating* is the obvious verb form for *narrative*. It loses something in the translation from noun to verb, and what we believe it loses is the simple, unsophisticated humanity of the person telling the story. Second, we unabashedly acknowledge the emotional connotations of the word *story* when contrasted with the word *narrative*. We stand with McEwan who declares that a story "deals not just in facts or ideas of theories, or even dreams, fears, and hopes, but in facts, theories, and dreams from the perspective of someone's life and in the context of someone's emotions" (McEwan 1995, xiii).

Pink, who argues that we are moving from an "information age" to a "conceptual age" in which right-brained aptitudes for intuition and emotion will complement if not be more important than left-brained aptitudes for logic and reason, sees stories as one remedy for information overload. "When facts become so widely available and instantly accessible, each one becomes less valuable," he writes. "What begins to matter more is the ability to place these facts in *context* and to deliver them with *emotional impact*" [emphasis Pink's] (Pink 2005, 101). "Creators and empathizers," "pattern recognizers," and "meaning makers," rather than "knowledge workers" (Pink 2005, 49–50), continues Pink, are the wave of the future. To what else but storytelling is Pink referring when he lists context, emotional impact, pattern recognizing, and meaning making? "When our lives are brimming with information and data," he continues, "it's not enough to marshal an effective argument. Someone somewhere will inevitably track down a counterpoint or rebut your point. The essence of persuasion, communication, and self-understanding has become the ability also to fashion a compelling narrative" (Pink 2005, 65–66).

Recently, the popular media and the Internet have witnessed a resurgence in storytelling, for instance, in National Public Radio's *Story Corps* and even the constant updates to the millions of blogs and other online social networking tools we use to try to establish connections between ourselves and others in this harried, confusing, often terrifying world. "Every life," writes Kearney, "is in search of a narrative. We all seek, willy-nilly, to introduce some kind of concord into the everyday discord and dispersal we find about us" (Kearney 2002, 4).

Stories have always had a place in academic creative writing classes, and thinkers and scholars since Aristotle have studied literary texts as narrative. With growing attention to "the narrative turn" among academics, however, the subject of narrative has gained further credibility as a subject of scholarly research. "The narrative turn" denotes the sea change in the study of the narrative that began to take place in the mid-1970s when scholars began to examine not just literary texts as narratives, but written and nonwritten discourse across many disciplines. Medical patient interviews, anthropological ethnographic research reports, court transcripts, and anecdotes recorded in business settings all have become fodder for study. Who is speaking, who is listening, what words are used, what is not being said or not being recorded all have become significant. Attention has swept across the disciplines from those that might be expected to evidence interest in the topic (literature, linguistics, film, and theater) to the social sciences (history, political science, sociology, anthropology, and others) to law and the health sciences.

Charon, for example, has created a program in Medical Narrative at Columbia where she trains physicians and medical students to become better listeners to the narratives being told by their patients. "Only in the telling is the suffering made evident" (Charon 2004, 862), she writes. If physicians will become more aware of the ways in which patients construct themselves through the words they choose and the ways in which they put those words together, medical treatment can become both more humane and more effective. A study using this kind of approach by Werner, Isaksen, and Malterud examined medical narratives of ten women with chronic muscle pain who frequently were treated as if their symptoms were psychosomatic. They point out that not only do their stories help them construct their realities as individuals, their stories help to constitute them as an often unwilling community of illness to which they do not want to belong and the other members of which they do not want to be associated with. Summarizing the results of their study of the discursive patterns of these patients, the authors conclude, "Through their accounts they both relate to and try to avoid the medical discourse about 'unexplained' pain, which some have described as 'fashionable diagnoses' or 'the present-day answer to hysteria'" (Werner, Isaksen, and Malterud 2004, 1043). Charon also believes that when doctors take time to tell their own stories they "render . . . whole that which they observe and undergo . . . [and] reveal transcendent truths, exposed in the course of illness, about ordinary human life" (Charon 2004, 862).

In a different discipline, sociology, Vinitzky-Seroussi (2001) examined the "narrative" embodied by the Israeli school ceremonies that commemorated Yitzhak Rabin's assassination. Vinitzky-Seroussi discovered that the question of whether and how to mark such a complicated violent attack against a single person rather than the Jewish state was politically fraught because of general disagreement about Rabin's leadership. By examining the solutions that the Israeli government arrived at, the author in effect read the sociopolitical narrative and concluded that the government solution had excluded that conflict as an important frame of reference and in so doing had set the stage for possible future conflicts.

Pagnucci, however, appears to dispute the newfound respectability of the narrative within the university, claiming, "The more trained in academic writing we are the further away from stories/narrative we move. The clarity, the delight, the pleasure, and the meaning making that can be found in stories, these are to be left to children" (Pagnucci 2004, 43). Can serious academic work and delightful meaning making coexist? The work of one of our colleagues in our College of Education and Human Ecology illustrates how they can.

Our colleague, a professor of education and a participant in one of our digital storytelling workshops, has been devoting his research to how drama and play in the elementary classroom can be the foundations of inquiry-based learning. Involving the teacher and his students in such dramatic play leads to richer outcomes on both sides. He had given scholarly conference presentations and written peer-reviewed journal articles about how elementary school-aged children's literacy skills could be developed by appealing to their imaginations and their natural love of play. Similarly, children's ethical dispositions could be developed "by enacting what we imagine" (Edmiston 2000, 68) about how our actions might affect others. But had he ever told his own personal story about being a member of the classroom? How might that kind of a story, with all its attendant humor and even pathos, appeal in a different way to a conference audience? Telling such a story might involve some risk of looking unscholarly or even foolish, so it involved some courage on his part to step away from the narrative and into the story. That he has been able to tell his personal story in graduate seminars and at conferences through use of a digital story he created while still being able to present the narrative of his scholarly research in the same setting illustrates how scholarship and joy or play can coexist, that stories can find a place within the larger narratives of the university.

Still, stories never have seemed a legitimate means of expression for academic libraries. The library, often referred to as "the heart of the university," seems to have no heart of its own. We would suggest this may be attributable to the fact that the library has lost its ability to tell stories, if it ever enjoyed that ability at all.

The dryness of the *Oxford English Dictionary* (2007) definitions of *story* notwithstanding, they do suggest important qualities of stories as we will discuss them that make storytelling relevant to today's academic library. That is, they "record the events in the life" of a community, in our case the community both within the library and the various external communities to which we extend ourselves. Furthermore, they can "amuse and interest," not merely edify, the listener. Edifying library users is an unquestioned part of a research library's mission, but amusement and interest are rarely if ever mentioned. Imagine, however, the new relationship between the library and its users if amusement and interest were encouraged.

Something not mentioned in the *Oxford English Dictionary* that is crucial to our definition is the often subtle and nuanced power of stories to evoke emotion in both the teller and the listener and thus to forge bonds of community between them. In 1936, the German philosopher Walter Benjamin lamented, "Less and less frequently do we encounter people with the ability to tell a tale properly. More and more often there is embarrassment all around when the wish to hear a story is expressed. It is as if something that seemed inalienable to us, the securest among our possessions, were taken from us: the ability to exchange experiences" (Benjamin 1968, 83). That "ability to exchange experiences" is the linchpin of this book.

For Benjamin, stories are gifts given by the storyteller and incorporated into the lives of the listeners: "The storyteller takes what he tells from his experiences—his own or that reported by others. And he in turn makes it the experience of those who are listening to his tale" (Benjamin 1968, 87).

There it is—a simple connection between one human being and another—a storyteller, a listener, and a story that connects them. That is, a story is not a story at all unless the storyteller shares it and the listeners receive it as their own. Stories never are just poured into the listener's head as the listener sits dumbly. Even a boring story, or a good story told without affect, inspires some reaction in the listener, such as, "Something sort of like that happened to me last week, but my story was a lot funnier. My boss must be the worst boss ever. Let me tell you about the memo he sent out."

More important to our discussion of digital storytelling in the academic library than differentiating between "story" and "narrative" (terms which we in fact will use interchangeably) will be our focus on Benjamin's "exchange of experiences" (Benjamin 1968, 83) through stories. Therefore, our definition of story in the academic library environment will focus on the development of community through the emotional connections brought about by a unified narration of a series of events—a story.

WHY TELL STORIES?

At their most fundamental level, the stories that others tell us and that we tell ourselves help us construct our own individual identities (Jacobs 2002), who we have been, who we are, and who we want to be. I grew up in a Chicago suburb, so am I a Chicagoan or a suburbanite? The answer—or answers—to that question may depend on the stories I have heard told about Chicago and about Chicago's North Shore, as well as the stories I have told myself. The stories, true or not, that I have heard (and constructed) about Chicago paint a much grittier, down-to-earth picture than the stories that constructed my more privileged North Shore life. Do I ultimately choose Chicago or North Shore? The choice probably will depend on a combination of the reality of what I experienced as I grew up on the North Shore and an invented story of who I want to be. Similarly, my identity as an American has been at least partially constructed by stories about my father fighting in World War II, my experiences protesting the Vietnam War, witnessing the planes crashing into the World Trade Center, and many, many more stories all told to me by others, such as my father, or constructed by me from my own experiences.

Every experience we have, theorize Schank and Berman (2002), becomes a story about that kind of experience. We file those stories away in our memory, categorizing them in order to add to those categories as we encounter similar experiences. We constantly refine and differentiate those categories, building our understanding of the world and our place in it into a more complex and sophisticated whole. So actually my identity is not as simplistic as a choice between being either from Chicago or from the North Shore. Rather, when I remember how I used to walk across the Loop every day to my summer job, having ridden the train downtown from my house on the North Shore; smell the restaurant exhaust fans blowing into the alleys; and hear the scream of the "El" trains above my head, my sense of myself as a Chicagoan grows. When I retell the story about how on a hot July afternoon a fellow secretary opened the window and jumped, my depth of understanding of how naive my suburban life was deepens.

All of our individual identities combine with others' to form various communal relationships. These range from bonds of family, neighborhood, sexual orientation, race, ethnic group, religion, nation, and more. When communities construct and share their stories, they construct a common history, bringing order and meaning to the otherwise "haphazard happenings of history" (Kearney 2002, 3).

Family stories about births, vacations, graduations, and weddings, home-leavings, and homecomings all help mothers, fathers, siblings, cousins and beyond develop the bonds of identity that form nuclear and extended family units of all stripes. In my family, for instance, the story of the night he was born has become an annual birthday ritual for my older son who is now thirty years old. He may wince when I launch into the telling, but should we forget this ritual he would miss it, so much a part of the fabric of our family has it become.

The stories that form the basis of religions are one example of the wider social, communal relationship agency that in fact may underlie a society's moral code. "We discover the self through a community's narrated tradition," writes Hauerwas (1983, 28). It is no accident, he claims, that tenets of Christian morality often are conveyed in the form of stories. Continuous repetition of a colorful tapestry of biblical stories and church history point the way to socially beneficial behavior that puts the community's needs before the individual's needs. This is an example of the dynamic relationship that Jacobs (2002) describes between personal stories and community stories. That is, while individual stories and identities combine to define the group's identity, the group's collective story in turn influences group members' individual identities.

Stories' ability to inspire moral action is not simply because of the way they instantiate traditional beliefs and codes but because of their capability of arousing empathy in the listener (Pinker and Goldstein 2005). Stories challenge our assumptions about other people's realities and force us to see things from other perspectives (Witherell, Tran, and Othus 1995). If I have been raised in a middle-class suburb, a story about a single mother trying to raise her children in a poor urban neighborhood may help create much deeper understanding in me than perusing decontextualized census tables of statistics about wages, child care, and family structures. Not that those statistics are not meaningful, but they become much more meaningful once my heart has been opened by a story told by someone who has lived the life being depicted by those statistics. This empathic connection with the other promotes a deeper morality than that with which I began. Strange cites as an example of this phenomenon the overwhelming effect that Harriet Beecher Stowe's *Uncle Tom's Cabin* had in marshalling support against slavery. Unlike other nineteenth-century writers who contended that the response to the novel was attributable to the volume of new information it conveyed, Strange quotes Charles Dudley Warner as citing its ability to "'go to the heart,' to strike 'the public conscience' and, ultimately, 'to carry the sort of conviction that results in action'" (Strange 2002, 263). Part of this effect of "going to the heart" may be due to what Polichak and Gerrig term the "participatory nature of audience response" (Polichak and Gerrig 2002, 73) to stories. Rather than merely being receptacles for stories, the listener is caught up in an interior "conversation" (Polichak and Gerrig 2002, 72) that evokes feelings, aids in remembering, and may even inspire action.

White believes that stories may aid in intercultural understanding as well. Narrative may be a "metacode" (White 1980, 2) that can be understood by people in other cultures even if those cultures do not understand location-specific codes such as rules, customs, and traditions. If not universally understandable, then at least stories are more likely to be understood from one culture to another. For instance, the story of the hero's journey away from home, through an initiation of some kind, and back home again is one common to most cultures.

Even corporations have used storytelling to build community in a thoughtful and intentional way. The communities they seek to influence include not only their customers but also their employees. The IBM online archives, for example, have a whole *Music Chronology* page that chronicles through song, symphony, and performance the story of IBM from 1915 through 2001. Another page, *The Way We Wore: A Century of IBM Attire* tells the different version of the same chronicle through the use of still photos. Both Web sites provide a nostalgic look backward at the history of IBM, reinforcing corporate identity through history and memory. Krispy Kreme has a vice-president whose duties include being the company "Story Master." Pink (2005) notes that Xerox has decided that the stories repair personnel tell each other are so much more valuable than a simple repair manual that they have collected those stories into what has been determined to be a multimillion dollar database. On the other hand, corporate leaders may tell stories to their sales forces to inspire devotion to the company and motivate behavior in desired directions. Furthermore, we all are familiar with staff lounge gossip that uses stories to build solidarity *against* the organization and thus perhaps helps individuals maintain their own identities rather than being totally subsumed by the corporate identity.

Corporations also frequently use stories in their advertising to humanize themselves to their customers. Consider how Wendy's used the story of the late Dave Thomas' adoption to put a human face on the company. Think of the many insurance companies that tell stories about the night the agent braved the aftermath of a tornado to offer not just financial but emotional support to her client, or of the pharmacist who tells the story about the old lady who came to town to visit her daughter but forgot to bring her blood pressure medication with her. Home Depot is now inviting customers to send in stories about how projects using the company's products and expertise have changed their lives, such as the divorced mother who single-handedly remodeled the home she bought for her daughters and herself. All of these exemplify corporations reaching out to their customers by means of storytelling.

In addition to creating relationships between and among individuals and groups, stories can explain and thus help construct knowledge and aid in sense-making. Like Pink, Sax (2006) believes that stories help us control the welter of information that bombards our senses. She sees numerous advantages of stories for purposes of meaning-making over such things as rules and formulas; for instance, stories involve the senses, and the minimal tools required are the teller's voice and the listener's ear.

By sorting the experiences of a first crush into a narrative a mother can help her son understand how adolescent girls think about boys. A story about a dog tied to a tree on a blazingly hot summer day can construct a listener's understanding, not just of the dog's reality, but of any creature, including human beings, whose freedom is restricted. Sharing a story about a wife's terminal illness with a friend can help a husband decide how to help her through her final days. Turning instruction in changing a tire into a story about one's first clumsy experience on a dark road in the middle of the night may prove more effective than a lecture, as will a story about seeing a homeless person sharing his money with another person on the bus possibly help develop a spirit of charity in one's children.

Stories, of course, do not have to be true. Selectivity about what details to include and in what order almost always guarantees some degree of license with the truth. Such divergence is hardly a negative characteristic because, as Hauerwas points out, such stories can in fact not just depict but "create reality" (Hauerwas 1983, 25).

Stories also provide us with the ability to look both backward and forward, to remember and to predict (Sunwolf and Frey, 2001). Remembering in order to build a common history and traditions contributes to building community. We build a family identity by remembering those shared holidays, graduations, vacations, and other more and less significant events. The story of the pilgrims celebrating the first Thanksgiving with the Indians may be a cliché of American history, but it is nevertheless an icon of American culture that binds many Americans together. Do you remember where you were when President Kennedy was assassinated, or when the World Trade Towers fell? The stories you tell in response to these questions contribute to the construction of a common American history.

Every time a corporate leader tells a story at an annual meeting in order to motivate company employees about the company's bright future, that leader is forecasting the future by using stories. Notes Benjamin (2006), case studies are a form of looking backward, while scenarios allow organizations to look into the future and forecast what would happen "if." Case studies traditionally have been used both in business schools and in company training programs "to define and validate present behaviors" (Benjamin 2006, 161). Incorporating personal stories into case stories, as Benjamin does at Mercy College, allows students to amplify their leadership skills through storytelling. She compares creating forward-looking scenarios to the parables of Jesus, claiming that "[m]uch like ancient prophesies and modern science fiction, scenarios are case studies that project a new vision of potential future realities" (Benjamin 2006, 162). Thus, stories in the corporate environment are an important way to humanize looking backward and looking forward, especially important in an age in which technology threatens to define human beings, rather than the other way around.

Lest we push the storytelling pendulum too far in the direction of sense-making, Gabriel reminds us that we should not forbid stories simply to entertain us. His point is well-taken. A story's memorability often is bestowed at least partially by its element of playfulness. "Postmodernist discourses have privileged stories and storytelling as sense-making devices; in so doing, many have lost sight of the qualities of storytelling as entertainment and challenge, and have blurred the boundaries between stories and other types of narratives, including interpretations, theories, and arguments" (Gabriel 2000, 19).

In a different vein, Gargiulo (2005) emphasizes stories' abilities both to hurt and to heal. Depending on the teller, the listener, the relationship between them, and the story being told, one can easily imagine a number of such scenarios. The popular media recently has told its own story of "mean girls," as young as elementary school age, who spread destructive stories about other girls over the Internet or through text messaging, sometimes leading to depression, eating disorders, and even suicide. Although scholarly discussion of this phenomenon is much more nuanced, it does serve as an easily imagined example of stories with the power to hurt. At the other end of the spectrum, stories with healing power are told every day in support groups for people suffering from cancer, alcoholism, or the burden of caring for a loved one with Alzheimer's. Hearing others who are enduring similar experiences tell their stories can bestow needed hope and strength upon the listener.

Perhaps Hernadi summarizes our need for stories best when he writes, "Stories and histories and other narrative or descriptive accounts help us to *escape boredom and indifference* [emphasis Hernadi's]—ours as well as that of other people. Those nearly vacant states of mind at the zero degree of entertainment and commitment bring us frightfully close to the experience of nonexistence" (Hernadi 1980, 199). Stories construct our individual identities and the identities of the communities, big and small, to which we belong. They inspire empathy that informs our sense of morality. They help us make sense of the information with which we are bombarded every day and from which we construct our knowledge and our worldview. Stories stand for our memories of the past and our vision of the future. They entertain us, and they help us entertain others. They can be used to hurt others, but they also can be used to heal. Do not fear the "messiness" or "unruly answers" that stories can sometime convey, urges Pagnucci (2004, 52–53), but rather embrace them for all the opportunities they offer.

REFERENCES

Benjamin, B. (2006). The case study: Storytelling in the industrial age and beyond. *On the Horizon,* 14, 159–164.

Benjamin, W. (1968). The storyteller: Reflections on the works of Nikolai Leskov. In H. Arendt (Ed.), *Walter Benjamin: Illuminations* (pp. 83–109). New York: Harcourt, Brace & World.

Charon, R. (2004). Narrative and medicine [electronic version]. *New England Journal of Medicine,* 350, 862–864.

Edmiston, B. (2000). Drama as ethical education [electronic version]. *Research in Drama Education,* 5, 63–84.

Gabriel, Y. (2000). *Storytelling in organizations: Facts, fictions, and fantasies.* New York: Oxford University Press.

Gargiulo, T. L. (2005). *The strategic use of stories in organizational communication and learning.* Armonk, NY: M.E. Sharpe.

Hauerwas, S. (1983). *The peaceable kingdom: A primer in Christian ethics*. Notre Dame, IN: University of Notre Dame Press.

Hernadi, P. (1980). On the how, what, and why of narrative. In W. J. T. Mitchell (Ed.), *On narrative* (pp. 197–199). Chicago, IL: University of Chicago Press.

International Business Machines (IBM). (n.d.). *Music chronology*. Retrieved February 28, 2007, from http://www-03.ibm.com/ibm/history/exhibits/music/music_CH1.html.

————. (n.d.). *The way we wore: A century of IBM attire*. Retrieved February 28, 2007, from http://www-03.ibm.com/ibm/history/exhibits/waywewore/waywewore_1.html.

Jacobs, R. N. (2002). The narrative integration of personal and collective identity in social movements. In M. C. Green., J. J. Strange, and T. C. Brock (Eds.), *Narrative impact: Social and cognitive foundations* (pp. 205–228). Mahwah, NJ: Lawrence Erlbaum.

Kearney, R. (2002). *On stories*. New York: Routledge.

Kreiswirth, M. (2000). Merely telling stories? Narrative and knowledge in the human sciences. *Poetics Today*, 21, 293–318.

McEwan, H. and Egan K. (Eds.). (1995). *Narrative in teaching, learning, and research*. New York: Teachers College Press.

National Public Radio. (n.d.). *StoryCorps*. Retrieved May 21, 2007, from http://www.npr.org/templates/story/story.php?storyId=4516989.

Oxford English Dictionary Online. (March 15, 2007). Retrieved April 11, 2007, from http://dictionary.oed.com/entrance.dtl.

Pagnucci, G. S. (2004). *Living the narrative life: Stories as a tool for meaning making*. Portsmouth, NH: Boynton/Cook.

Pink, O. H. (2005). *A whole new mind: Moving from the information age to the conceptual age*. New York: Riverhead Books.

Pinker, S. and Goldstein, R. (2005). The seed salon (no. 2). *Seed Magazine*. Retrieved July 12, 2005, from http://www.seedmagazine.com/?p=article&id=100000020&cp=0.

Polichak, J. W. and Gerrig, R. A. (2002). Get up and win!: Participatory responses to narrative. In M. C. Green, J. J. Strange, and T. C. Brock (Eds.), *Narrative impact: Social and cognitive foundations* (pp. 71–96). Mahwah, NJ: Lawrence Erlbaum.

Sax, B. (2006). Storytelling and the "information overload." *On the Horizon*, 14, 165–170.

Schank, R. C. and Berman, T. R. (2002). The pervasive role of stories in knowledge and action. In M. C. Green, J. J. Strange, and T. C. Brock (Eds.), *Narrative impact: Social and cognitive foundations* (pp. 287–314). Mahwah, NJ: Lawrence Erlbaum.

Stein, N. L. and Kissel, V. L. (2005). Story schemata and causal structure. In D. Herman, M. Jahn, and M. Ryan (Eds.), *Routledge encyclopedia of narrative theory* (pp. 568–569). New York: Routledge.

Strange, J. J. (2002). How fictional tales wag real-world beliefs: Models and mechanisms of narrative influence. In M. C. Green, J. J. Strange, and T. C. Brock (Eds.), *Narrative impact: Social and cognitive foundations* (pp. 263–286). Mahwah, NJ: Lawrence Erlbaum.

Sunwolf and Frey, L. R. (2001). Storytelling: The power of narrative communication and interpretation. In P. W. Robinson and H. Giles (Eds.), *The new handbook of language and social psychology* (pp. 119–135). New York: John Wiley & Sons.

Vinitzky-Seroussi, V. (2001). Commemorating narratives of violence: The Yitzhak Rabin Memorial Day in Israeli schools [electronic version]. *Qualitative Sociology*, 24, 245–268.

Werner, A., Isaken, L. W. and Malterud, K. (2004). "I am not the kind of woman who complains of everything": Illness stories on self and shame in women with chronic pain [electronic version]. *Social Science and Medicine*, 59, 1035–1045.

White, H. (1980). The value of narrativity in the representation of reality. In W. J. T. Mitchell (Ed.), *On narrative* (pp. 1–23). Chicago: University of Chicago Press.

Witherell, C. with Tran, H. T., and Othus, J. (1995). Narrative landscapes and the moral imagination: Taking the story to heart. In H. McEwan and K. Egan (Eds.), *Narrative in teaching, learning, and research* (pp. 39–49). New York: Teachers College Press.

CHAPTER 2

What Is a Digital Story?

THE ELEMENTS OF A DIGITAL STORY

A digital story is simply a movie made using some combination of digitized still images, video clips, voiceover narration, and music. For several reasons, which we will discuss later in this chapter, digital stories tend to be short, usually only three- to five-minutes long. The list of required and optional hardware and software is relatively short:

- Computer (preferably with a DVD burner)
- Digital camera
- Scanner
- USB microphone
- Photo-editing software (for instance, iPhoto or Photoshop)
- Sound-recording software (for instance, Sound Studio, GarageBand, or Audacity)
- Video-editing software (for instance, iMovie or Adobe Premier)
- Optional: digital video camera, headphones, sound-mixing board

Digital storytelling, as we describe it here, was conceptualized in the 1990s by the late Dana Atchley who with Joe Lambert and Nina Mullen went on to found the Center for Digital Storytelling (CDS) in Berkeley, California. Today the CDS offers workshops both on- and off-site to teach people how to create digital stories and to train others to extend the Center's work. The CDS has collaborated with organizations as diverse as the British Broadcasting Corporation (BBC), the National Gallery of Art, and the Kansas City Symphony.

In *Digital Storytelling: Capturing Lives, Creating Community*, Lambert (2002) lists "the seven elements" of digital storytelling: "point (of view), dramatic question, emotional content, the gift of your voice, the power of the soundtrack, economy, and pacing" (Lambert 2002, xi).

Lambert conflates point and point of view to describe two different aspects of storytelling. The point of a story is the author's overall goal, or why this story is important for the author to tell at this moment in her life; for example, "I want my mother to know that I now understand how hard it must have been to deal with me when I was a teenager;" or, "I want to introduce the first year students to the treasures in our Rare Book Collection."

The story's point is more specific than the subject of the story. For a storyteller to state that her subject is the bewilderment of parents of teenagers actually starts her on the path of not fully engaging with her listener. It allows her to limit herself to a one-sided abstraction that overemphasizes the "I," as in "I want to talk about the experience of being a parent. (And I really don't care who is listening.)" If, on the other hand, the storyteller states the point of her story in terms of what she hopes to share with her listener, she is much farther along the road to engaging personally with that listener. The story with a point connects a teller and a listener; for instance, a daughter with a mother, a librarian with first year students, or a CEO with employees.

The storyteller has many choices to make among points of view from which to tell her story, and that choice will be crucial to the overall impact of the story. The choice of point of view will be determined in part by the point the teller is trying to make. The storyteller's options may include: Am I a daughter talking to my mother, or am I a woman talking to another woman? Or am I a daughter who is now a woman, talking to my mother who is also a woman? Will I use the first person or second person, or third person voice?

Listen to the difference:

First person: "Now that I have kids of my own, I realize how selfish I was."
Second person: "You must have wanted to cry on Mother's Day."
Third person: "She often wonders how her mother felt that Mother's Day."

The first person version places more emphasis on the speaker's new self-awareness. The second person version projects herself into her mother's place, perhaps creating a stronger connection between the two women. The third person, while expressing a willingness to project herself into her mother's place, nevertheless maintains some distance.

Another question relating to point of view is from what time perspective the storyteller will tell the story. The obvious answer is to look backward, but it is also possible to look forward in order to wonder, "What if?" Examples from the CDS workshop we attended in Asheville, North Carolina, in 2005 illustrate both of these possibilities. One workshop participant remembered her trip to China to adopt her daughter. She had been prepared for some initial shyness on the little girl's part, but had never dreamed she would spend two weeks in a Chinese hotel with a three-year-old who never smiled. Toys, ice cream, songs, and warm blankets—none of these elicited a glimmer of a smile. "Will my daughter ever smile for me?" she had wondered. Pictures taken later of a happy six-year-old, secure in her new home in America, provided our answer. On the other hand, another participant, a nineteen-year-old young man, used his story to describe the kind of work environment in which he thrived in order to forecast the kind of career he thought he might choose.

The storyteller also has the choice of which elements to reveal and which to keep hidden, as if saying to the listener, "I'm only going to reveal enough about this subject to tantalize you. I want to make you want to find out more about this manuscript that is one of the treasures of this special collection." He may even want to assume the guise of someone who is exploring and discovering the details of the story along with his listener.

The story's dramatic question, whether explicit or implicit, might be compared to the journalist's "hook" that draws the listener into the story. It brings both the story's point and its point of view into focus for the listener, keeping the listener involved from beginning to end. The dramatic question may be revealed in the very first sentence of the narration or it may only be suggested by the background music or a key image. Here are some dramatic questions that we have seen drive digital stories in our workshops: What does my daughter's name mean? What do gold earrings signify about my own girlhood in Sierra Leone, and what does my daughter's choice of earrings signify about her own growing up as an American? What did those red ink markings on my student's leg mean? In another story, the storyteller drew her listeners in by keeping them wondering to whom she was speaking in her story.

The emotional content of the digital story distinguishes these stories from a mere recitation of the day's activities to a colleague or a public relations video distributed by a library's communications office. The emotions conveyed by the story can run the gamut from delight to melancholy to horror. Sometimes digital stories even may evoke tears. That storytelling invites the teller to reveal his emotions and in turn evoke an emotional response in his audience is one reason why it may seem so inappropriate in the academic setting. It is one crucial factor, however, in establishing a connection between the storyteller and the listener. In the traditionally text-based, left-brained library environment, acknowledging the emotional potential of stories and permitting those emotions to be expressed within the library environment is perhaps one of the biggest leaps that librarians have to make.

Appropriately labeled by Lambert as a "gift" (Lambert 2002, xi), the teller's own spoken voice in the digital story provides a wealth of information to the listener. Rather than listening to a neutralized voiceover actor, the listener hears a flesh and blood person whose voice suggests that she is a woman, possibly elderly, perhaps African American, probably from somewhere in the South. Maybe it is the voice of a child, or an aging veteran. Hearing that voice, the listener begins to form a picture of the storyteller that deepens, intensifies and enriches the meaning of the story.

In workshops in which we have participated we have heard collective groans when participants are told they will need to record their own voices. A library student assistant from Japan, whose English is completely understandable, recently announced that he was just going to leave his voice out altogether so much did he hate to listen to himself. We think it would be a fascinating experiment to have two different people read the voiceover to the same movie. Depending on the story and the voices, we expect that the stories might elicit quite different responses from the listeners. The whole point of the story might be perceived differently.

The insurance company that presents a famous voice alongside an average person who is telling her own story makes the point of how important the gift of voice is. In one television commercial, a housewife recounts how her family's Thanksgiving dinner was almost ruined by a flood in her basement. "Mashed potaaaaatoes!" sings Little Richard, sitting beside her providing color commentary. In another, a voiceover actor stands behind a woman in her kitchen and retells her story in counterpoint to her telling it. The redundancy of his voiceover, and the fact that we can clearly see and hear that he is a man at a microphone with his hand to his ear provides incomparable testimony to the power of her voice, not his.

Imagine *Schindler's List* without John Williams' music or *American Graffiti* without its '50s and '60s collage of rock and roll hits to carry you back into that era. This is the "power of the soundtrack" (Lambert 2002, xi) to which Lambert refers. Digital stories certainly can be told without music—and there may be times when the very absence of music speaks eloquently—but in general, music adds another layer to the story that enhances mood, builds emotion, and even can tell part of the story. One of our colleagues, for example, is working on a digital story about swing dancing to use in a conversational English class with Chinese students. While swing music as soundtrack obviously is appropriate to the story, it also serves the very practical purpose of providing a shorthand description of swing music for people from other cultures.

Because digital stories are so short, usually just three to five minutes long, the storyteller has to be economical. That is, he must spend every word wisely, as if each one were his last penny. Equivocation and redundancy have no place here, and everything learned in freshman composition about writing concisely comes into play. Fortunately, images and soundtrack can help the storyteller in this regard with a picture becoming literally worth a thousand words. The French have an expression *le mot juste*, which means *the perfect word*. Choosing the word *chalice* instead of *large silver cup* produces the desired picture in a single, specific word, denoting as well its sacred character. As Lambert (2002) points out, juxtaposed images and sound provide another and richer text to be heard and interpreted by the listener.

Finally, even the shortest digital story can bore its audience or waste its potential impact if the storyteller does not pace it effectively. Variations in speed, rhythm, and intensity of the narrator's voice, the music, and the presentation of images all matter. That is, does the narrator pause, does she repeat key phrases, does the music become louder or softer, does the story occasionally cut quickly between images or use slow fades or even some black space between them?*

AN EXAMPLE FROM THE LIBRARY

While the digital story format is particularly well-suited to stories about one's life outside the working world, we have come to believe that the seven elements can be incorporated into stories about libraries, as well. For example, an archivist at our institution created a digital story about her involvement with a historical cartoon collection that demonstrated all seven of these elements. The point of the story was to make visible to the world this somewhat hidden collection. The story was told from the point of view of one who knew intimately every inch of the

716 linear feet of materials dating from 1894 to 1996 that comprised the San Francisco Academy of Comic Art Collection of newspaper comic strips purchased by Ohio State University in 1997 from collector William Blackbeard. Her dramatic question was, why would I take on a task as daunting as trying to organize a collection of over 2.5 million newspaper clippings, comic pages, and newspapers? The emotion that her story clearly conveyed was her passion for preserving the cultural history embodied in these materials, yet the tone of her voice was nostalgic, with a slight Georgia lilt to it. An old piano-roll rag played in the background, establishing without words the time period of some of the more colorful comics. While she lingered on some images to lure her audience into the collection, she varied the pacing of the story by increasing the speed between cuts as she showed images of the tractor-trailers that were required to ship the collection from California to Ohio. This story exemplifies not only all seven elements of a digital story, but also one possible application of the form in a library setting.

THE PROCESS OF CREATING A DIGITAL STORY

Products like Apple's iLife suite make moviemaking something people can learn on their own in their own homes. There is more to making a story, however, than using the technology. Furthermore, until one develops facility with the technology, producing a movie can take many hours of work, both during and beyond the scheduled hours of a story workshop. Having participated in and now facilitated several workshops ourselves, however, we still believe that the time is well worth it. Rewards grow as the learning curve declines with every iteration of the workshop process.

The digital storytelling workshops facilitated by the CDS run for three full days and incorporate all the steps required for producing a finished story. We have tried variations on the three-day theme at our institution, something we will discuss later in the book. Regardless of workshop format, however, the process of creating a digital story begins, not even with a completed script, but with an idea. Having a rough draft of a script in hand is helpful, but in most cases the story will pass through a number of revisions. Crucial to these revisions is the feedback obtained by sharing the story idea or script with others in what Lambert calls a "story circle" (Lambert 2002, 95). In the story circle all the participants take turns reading or describing their stories. Others in the group listen thoughtfully and offer constructive responses about directions in which the teller might profitably take her story. These first responses provide a helpful measure for the teller of where she has or has not connected with her potential audience. They may give the teller a better idea of where to begin or end the story, of how to weave two strands together, of what kinds of images or video clips to include, and what kind of musical background to create. Each person is given approximately fifteen minutes to present and then to converse with the group.

For instance, at a workshop sponsored by Ohio State University the education professor who was creating his digital story in order to personalize his research on the topic of imaginative inquiry found that his original script did just what he hoped it would not. It defined and explained imaginative inquiry, but it did not make the concept live and breathe. During the question and answer period that followed his reading, members of the group asked him some clarifying questions about his topic.

As a means of further explaining the concept he told a story. One day a little girl in the second grade class in which he was doing his research, who steadfastly had refused to join the class for a reading and discussion of "The Three Little Pigs," came and stood by the professor's side. She had red magic marker all over her leg. Why in the world had she done that, he wondered. The answer was obvious to her classmates: "The wolves got her!" Almost as one, the storytelling group exclaimed, "There's the beginning of your story!" He returned the next day with a new story. From the children's initial engagement with the drama of the wolves' attack on their classmate came days of planning and carrying out the relocation of Beanie-Baby wolves from the Little Pigs' habitat to a more wolf-friendly national park. With their imaginations fully engaged the children inquired into American geography, veterinary medicine, and the math required to calculate cross-country wolf-shipping costs.

The impulse to tell the story in order to explain the concept of imaginative inquiry to the group came naturally to our colleague, as we are convinced it does to all of us. The rest of the story seemed to flow almost effortlessly from the image of the little girl with the red magic marker on her leg. Learning the technology over the next two days took considerable effort, but the skeleton of the narrative was well in place, thanks to his collaboration with the story circle members.

We cannot overemphasize how important we believe the story circle is to the process of digital storytelling. The notion of story circle has larger implications beyond the fifteen-minute vetting of one's ideas, as Lambert (2002) points out. It also establishes the safe cocoon in which participants begin to feel free to share honestly with one another. Because everyone takes a turn, everyone shares the same risk and almost immediately comes to realize that everyone in the group is on equal footing. Some may be better at putting words together as text; others better at choosing images or creating video clips. Music may be others' strength. Having shared their stories from the very beginning, whether in an intensive three-day workshop or over the course of an academic term, story circle participants develop an authentic sense of community as they watch the germ of a story become a fully realized miniature jewel.

Safety and security involve the ability to limit how much people share of themselves, too. Sometimes a participant may bow out of the workshop when it seems that the emotions brought forth by working on a story are too intense. In some settings facilitated by the CDS the subject of the workshop is so emotionally charged, for instance by a shared history of domestic abuse, that the workshop leaders have had mental health professionals sit in on the story circle. Some people may tentatively sign up for a workshop, attend the story circle but hang back, waiting to see if they do feel comfortable with the group. As they watch the circle progress, they may develop enough confidence to join and share their story idea and ultimately to share their completed digital movie with the group. But for a variety of professional or personal concerns that must be respected by the group, they may decide that they do not want their movie to go beyond the confines of the group.

Whether the story must come before selecting the images is a debatable question. Having at least a rough script in place obviously can suggest appropriate images that will bring the script to life. The images can come from a wide range of sources. Old photos can be scanned into digital format, or original photos can be created digitally. Video clips also can be incorporated into the story. Photos can be downloaded from the Internet if they are in the public domain. Original artwork can be created digitally or manually and then photographed digitally.

Still photographs need to be readied for incorporation into the movie-editing software by manipulation with a photo-editing software package such as PhotoShop. Cropping, color and red-eye correction, transfer from color to black and white or sepia tones, and other techniques all can be used to help focus attention on important elements of the story. Black and white images, for instance, might be especially appropriate to a story that looks back several generations. Images can be superimposed upon other images, for instance a piece of tape over a woman's mouth to signify her silencing by her culture.

We have seen a collage of documents from the Holocaust used to dramatic effect as a workshop participant made the point that her mother's history consisted not of family pictures but of the words and symbols that transported her away from her home, conscripted her to work camps, or labeled her clothing. The collage our storyteller created was indeed created out of pictures, but they were all pictures of words and symbols, something that suited exceptionally well the story she was trying to tell about a woman whose identity and memories had been reduced from pictures to text.

It may be the case that sometimes creation of the story script grows organically from a collection of found images, rather than the images springing from the script or story idea. As with lyrics to a song that simply may cry out for a tune, a collection of images similarly may cry out for a story. One participant in a digital storytelling workshop at our university brought with her old eight-millimeter movie film that her father had made when he and his family had lived briefly in the Fiji Islands. Our storyteller had converted the old film to digital format in order to present DVD copies to her brothers and sisters, but she wanted to go further. She wanted to project herself into her father's imagination as he landed in that exotic new home for the first time, leaving behind the United States for an indeterminate amount of time. She actually had clips of the islands taken from the vantage point of the propeller airplane, along with the sound of the engines rushing in the background. The jerkiness of the film frames and their fuzzy focus only enhanced the sense that this was a story that had taken place in another time and was being imagined in a dreamlike state.

Imagine opening a trunk in your grandmother's attic and discovering a packet of old hand-painted postcards from your grandfather fastened together with fragile yellow satin ribbons. What story might the postcards ask you to tell? Moving into the realm of academic libraries, imagine that you opened a box of donated papers and discovered three letters written by Henry James. The sheer academic value of the letters notwithstanding, what stories might demand to be told about James' relationship to the letters' owner? (Think of James' short story "The Aspern Papers.") Even in the library's cataloging department, imagine the stories that might escape upon opening a drawer of an old wooden card catalog and running one's fingers through yellowed catalog cards marked with red ink and white typewriter erasing liquid.

Regardless of whether the image or the story script comes first, the best way to create the digital movie itself is to import your manipulated images and video clips into the movie-editing software package you will be using. There are several applications that accommodate images, voice, and soundtrack well such as Windows Movie Maker, Adobe Premier, or Adobe FinalCut Pro. Apple's iMovie, however, is considered one of the simpler applications for beginners to use. iMovie is part of the Apple iLife suite that comes loaded on every Macintosh computer. In iMovie you only need to import saved images and clips and then drag and drop them onto the video track of the movie. You then can easily manipulate them within iMovie in order to lengthen the time they are shown on the screen and create zoom, pan, specialized visual effects, title slides, and transitions.

Once the video images are roughly in place, it is time to create the voiceover narration that will be the first of two audiotracks, the second being the background music. A number of software packages exist for recording the script, for instance, GarageBand and Audacity. Garage-Band also is part of the Apple iLife suite. Minimally, you can plug in a simple USB microphone to the computer and record your narration. For better sound quality, however, you can record the voiceover through an inexpensive sound-mixing board that has its own power supply and thus generates higher quality sound. You can adjust sound levels using the sound-mixing board.

If using GarageBand, importing the completed voiceover into the digital story is a simple matter of "sharing" the voiceover into iTunes and then exporting it into iMovie. Once you have dragged and dropped the narration into your movie, you probably will want to spend some time synchronizing the images with the ideas of the voiceover. Here is one point in the creation of a digital story where pacing comes into play. Just as you want listeners to be able to make sense of the spoken words they are listening to, you will want to consider carefully how they will make sense of—or "read"—the images they are viewing on the screen.

Movie-editing software packages come with a wide array of special effects and transitions that you can apply, depending as always on the story being told. Beginners sometimes find it difficult to avoid the temptation to overuse some of these effects. Judicious use of a cross-dissolve, however, can enhance the idea of a little girl growing into an old woman. One visual effect can split a single image into multiples, one way of demonstrating exponential growth.

Creating and laying down a musical soundtrack is the final step in creating the digital story itself. If you want to share your story widely, for instance via the Internet, that music must be either original or copied from one of the several public domain music sites that exist on the Web, for instance, the Creative Commons. Creating your own music is even better. Music authoring software, such as Apple's GarageBand, offers a wealth of copyright-free musical clips representing many styles and instrumentations that you can combine into inventive musical scores for your movie. As with the voiceover, after creating the score, share and export it via iTunes, then drag and drop it into the movie as a second soundtrack. Within iMovie, adjust the volume and apply special audio effects as desired.

This is a good time to emphasize that the process that we describe, using Apple's iLife suite, is only one example of how a digital story can be created. Windows Movie Maker, Adobe's Premier and FinalCut Pro, Microsoft's PowerPoint and animated tutorial applications such as Captivate and Camtasia can be used to create inventive, engaging brief movies that accomplish the community-building that we see as the hallmark of digital stories in the academic library environment. Newer versions of Windows come with the movie-editing application called Movie Maker. Movie Maker's limitation is that it only has two tracks, one for video and one for audio. Overcoming this limitation is possible, however, by recording voice and background music as a single track and then importing that single audiotrack into Movie Maker.

Even at three to five minutes in length, these movies are huge files unless compressed appropriately when they are complete. Even without its music track, a three-minute movie can fill nearly an entire two-gigabyte flash drive. For students who depend on a university's computer labs for their digital media needs, the movies in development are not portable or even saveable unless they can be temporarily saved to a desktop or to an institutional server. Faculty and staff usually will be successful saving them to their own desktops or their assigned server space. Therefore, once the movies are completed and ready for viewing and distribution, they should be saved in a compressed format. The iMovie "share" function allows compression to Quicktime or CD format, both manageable sizes. The movies can be saved to DVDs or transferred to streaming video format and made available through a local institutional repository, as we are trying to do on our campus.

After the movies are finished, three important steps remain. First, showcase them among the workshop participants with whom you first undertook the story circle. It is difficult to overstate how moving it can be to view the final products of your workshop group with other group members and to see how inexperienced storytellers have taken an initial halting recitation of their story ideas and transformed them into fully realized movies. Everyone becomes an artist displaying talents they may never have dreamed they possessed. Therefore, it is important to allow time for this sharing with the small group.

Second, hold a showcase and invite the campus community at large. We have enjoyed wide attendance at the campus showcases we have held so far. Usually, the individual storytellers introduce their stories. Sometimes the audience members comment briefly or ask questions. We also have held showcases in more of an open-house format where movies are loaded on computers in a learning commons environment. Visitors browse the stories and the creators are available to hold conversations with the people who come by. Everyone attending seems genuinely moved by both the sometimes innocent artistry of the movies and the bravery of their creators. We have gleaned a number of participants for future workshops from these showcase sessions.

More importantly, in both the small group and campus showcases we see the start of community-building that undergirds our storytelling program in the first place. We learn things about colleagues whom we have known for a long time and colleagues whom we have only just met because of the workshops. We meet people who work in our own small department within the library, but we also meet people from campus units only distantly related to us by discipline, campus location, or mission.

Finally, make the digital stories available to the world on the Web. We have worked out a process for doing this through our institutional repository, the Ohio State University Knowledge Bank, that involves transforming the movies to streaming format and creating a handle in the institutional repository with a link to the university's streaming server.

DIGITAL STORYTELLING IN SOCIAL/CIVIC CONTEXTS

In a presentation to faculty and staff at the University of Maryland–Baltimore County, Lambert (2006) points out that creating individual, personal stories actually come fairly naturally to people because the process is rather like assembling an album out of family photos. Eventually, though, these small individual stories come to form a larger story of social units beyond the family. Although fairly new to the environment of higher education, digital storytelling has been widely used in social and civic contexts outside of academe. The significance of digital storytelling in a wider social context is described by Tharp and Hills who note that normally the stories of an indigenous culture have been recorded by outsiders. "These stories were told from a perspective that was not theirs, and could not possibly capture the full richness of the culture, because the tellers were not members of the particular culture and they brought their own external cultural biases and motivations into the interpretations" (Tharp and Hills 2004, 40). It is not so much that digital storytelling teaches people to use technology, they continue, but that it allows people to "take control of their own story, and tell it in a way that has not been possible before the advent of multimedia approaches that are now available to a much wider section of society" (Tharp and Hills 2004, 44). Friday morning listeners to National Public Radio's *StoryCorps* recordings have laughed and cried to audio stories told by fathers, daughters, sisters, and friends. A new initiative of *StoryCorps* is the *Griot Initiative*, which will collect stories nationwide from African Americans, especially World War II veterans and people who participated in the Civil Rights Movement.

The CDS, whose purpose in storytelling is to build community, has partnered with a wide variety of groups to bring digital storytelling to the community. One of their first projects was the *Capture Wales* project in collaboration with the BBC. *Capture Wales* set out to do just that, to capture stories from villages around Wales and in so doing preserve the culture of the country. Today the project is going strong, helping people from all over Wales tell their stories.

Other CDS projects have been devoted to preventing violence and promoting emotional healing in violent domestic relationships. These include the *Silence Speaks* and the *Bay Area Video Coalition/YouthLINK* projects. *Silence Speaks* not only allows victims of domestic violence to tell their stories, but is now working in South Africa to empower victims of AIDS to tell their stories. They also are working with day laborers in the San Francisco Bay area. The hope is that a variety of these stories can be used to influence public policy.

The goal of change typifies the purpose of many of the digital storytelling programs sponsored not only by the CDS but also by other similar training programs. *Stories for Change*, for example, is a coalition of storytelling consultants including the CDS, MassIMPACT, Creative Narrations, EduWeave, Storybuilders, and the Middlebury College Department of English. One Storybuilders project partnered Boston Public Health Commission employees with Boston University School of Public Health graduate students to train them to train community members in the process. They used *Google's* Picasa and Windows Movie Maker, two simple multimedia applications, to train community members to tell their own health-related stories. By using these stories in public discussions, the professionals hope to change the face of public health. More importantly, the community members themselves will have contributed to this effort. Professional and student participants in the workshops discovered that an added benefit of the workshops was that they met people from their own organizations whom they had never known before and deepened relationships with the people whom they had known before.

The Center for Reflective Community Practice at the Massachusetts Institute of Technology (MIT) and Creative Narrations, a storytelling consulting firm, also have partnered in using digital storytelling for community development. They have worked with the Boston Public Schools; a Roxbury, Massachusetts public housing project; and a Puerto Rican neighborhood advocacy group in Springfield, Massachusetts to bring about change in all those environments. In each project, as Marcuss describes them, the participants "have found an innovative way to voice their values by harnessing the power of digital media. Their successes are filling computer hard drives with a digital library of the sights, sounds, and voices of communities in action. It is a new anthology of community" (Marcuss 2007, 13).

Adobe's *Youth Voices* program funds various youth-based initiatives to encourage youth to mediate their worlds with technology. *Eduweave*, a member of the *Stories for Change* coalition, works with children and youth in developing countries, such as India, and underserved communities in developed countries who otherwise would not have access to technology. *Bridges to Understanding*, sponsored by Microsoft, uses digital storytelling "to connect people across cultures and see for a moment through someone else's eyes," connecting for example students from Seattle with students in South Africa to learn what South African students can teach American students about reconciliation.

With the *StoryMapping* project, the CDS now is moving into the realm of layering GPS-based tools with the multimedia tools of which it already has taken advantage. This project is combining narratives with specific places by using digital tools such as *Flickr* and *GoogleMaps* so that when a viewer clicks on a spot on a map a picture of that location will display and a story will be told. For instance, listeners may hear the grandson of the owner of the dry cleaners that used to be located on a particular corner tell a story about his memories of the store. This takes the concept of the audio walking tour one step beyond its current capabilities, perhaps the most important feature being that professional narrators are not telling the stories but rather the people with the actual memories of the stores, houses, parks, and movie theaters. One neighborhood the CDS is helping to capture is New Orleans' Central City neighborhood. The *I-10 Witness* project of New Orleans also has undertaken a story-mapping project to allow survivors of Hurricane Katrina to record their memories of New Orleans, both pre- and post-Hurricane Katrina.

The *Street Stories* project of the University of California–Berkley's Social Technologies Group is doing something similar, using hand-held devices to allow people to record stories wherever they want to. This project arose from the perception that "when people move elsewhere or (sub)urban development paves over an area, the stories are decoupled from the places and the places lose their vernacular particularities and are transformed into much more generic spaces. As increasing numbers of geographically based communities are displaced by network-based communities, the places of community—and their associated stories—are lost" (University of California–Berkley's Social Technologies Group 2007, para. 17).

Recently, various Web sites, both corporate and otherwise, have invited users to submit their own digital stories for viewing by the world and sometimes for the opportunity to win a prize. Home Depot has invited viewers to submit stories of how the life of their family or their community has been changed by their relationship with Home Depot. The prize was seeing their story told as a television commercial. *Librareo*, sponsored by Thomson-Gale, invited users to submit digital stories about libraries. The winner, who won a $10,000 cash prize to be shared with the library they had written about, was announced at the 2007 annual meeting of the American Library Association.

Commercial filmmakers are beginning to explore the form of short movies, intending them for downloading to cell phones. They have coined the term "Cellywood" for this new format, not feature length movies downloaded to cell phones but movies created particularly for display on the smallest of screens. A recent newscast that reported on this phenomenon showed as one example a Chihuahua with its hair in foils at a beauty salon and as another example a strange black-clad, techno-dancing foursome in a diner. In the background, underneath the counter a toddler dances along, too, as does the grizzled old short-order cook. So completely different were these films from each other that we could not help but imagine what a story circle would have been like that revolved around these storytellers. "I want to do a story about what it would be like for my dog to have a day at the spa." Who cares, we might have asked. The one with the dancers has more of the elements of a digital story, however. For instance, the dramatic question may be why are these dancers so completely out of context and why are they looking only at one another and not engaged with their surroundings? Yet why are those in the background, the toddler and the cook, so involved with the dance? As odd as the movie is we can see considerable potential for an interesting discussion on aesthetics, the relationship between art and society, and a number of other topics.

This brings us back to the story circle experience that we believe is so fundamental to the digital storytelling process if it is to maximize its potential. A story may entertain or move the viewer. Individuals certainly can put together wonderful digital stories in the comfort of their own homes as long as they have a computer and the appropriate software. Writing a story, selecting images, and combining them with a soundtrack leads to stories whose quality increases with the quantity of critical thinking applied to their production. But without the community of a story circle with whom to try out ideas, the experience of creation is diminished and, concomitantly we believe, the story may be diminished, as well. Stories created in the story circle environment have empowered participants in workshops sponsored by the CDS and other projects to change their lives and the lives of their families, friends, schools, and communities. This is a very different result than the result of a Cellywood video produced for its ability to explore technology, to entertain, and possibly to make money, but not to change the world.

OUR OWN FIRST EXPERIENCE WITH DIGITAL STORYTELLING

We first read about digital storytelling while we were participating in a summer study group in our library that was investigating trends in teaching and learning in university classrooms and libraries. Some of our reading about learning had interested us in the notion of multimodal projects as a means for students to demonstrate their learning. It occurred to us that student projects would be appropriate content to display on big-screen televisions that our library was planning to install in its renovated building. It also occurred to us that library staff had an ample supply of stories that they could tell multimodally and also display on those screens, as well as through the library's Web site, our institutional repository, and other venues.

We registered for a three-day digital storytelling workshop led by the CDS in Asheville, North Carolina in April, 2005. Most of the twelve participants planned to work individually, but a few of us worked as pairs. Participants ranged from high school teachers, to college students, to college professors, and we two librarians. All were instructed to come prepared with a script of no more than 250 words as well as images and music that we might want to include in our movies.

Although we knew that the CDS stresses personal digital stories, we wanted to tell a story about the three-year renovation our main library was about to undergo. We especially wanted to talk about how the library was moving toward becoming a library that emphasizes learning over teaching and that pays attention to the university's undergraduates. We brought with us pictures of the library and the campus; a script in which we tried to incorporate faculty, student, and librarian points of view; and a Larry Carlton jazz guitar CD.

Our group's subjects ranged from the weighty (a mother's transport to a Nazi concentration camp) to the sentimental (a thirtieth wedding anniversary) to the humorous (sweet iced tea). Even at that early stage in the workshop and without digital embellishment several stories drew tears in the story circle. Not ours. Our turn came last. Compared to everyone else's, our script was businesslike and lifeless, and we knew it. We were only grateful that no one laughed.

"If you really want to write about the library," Joe Lambert drawled, "I suppose that's all right. But I'd be interested in knowing what all these changes mean to you personally." So we returned to our hotel rooms and spent the whole evening thinking not about the library's story but our own story, and by the next morning we had transformed our script completely.

The next two days were a whirlwind of scanning photographs, learning photo- and video-editing applications, recording our scripts, and laying down our musical soundtracks. The workshop culminated nearly three hectic days after we had begun with showing all the final digital stories to each other. Almost everyone had taken comments from the story circle to heart and incorporated them into their final movies, often with dramatic results. A slight change in focus of the script, lingering on a particular photograph, or varying background music to change the tempo of the pacing brought remarkable poignancy to many of the stories that, only two days before, had been unfocused and incoherent. We had traveled to Asheville simply curious about the process of creating digital stories, but we returned home convinced that the form promised to allow the library to tell its stories in ways we had not anticipated. We were convinced that digital storytelling promised a means for the university community to tell the many, many stories that lay untapped and, in the telling, build community.

REFERENCES

Adobe Youth Voices. (March 30, 2007). Retrieved June 7, 2007, from http:// www.adobe.com/aboutadobe/philanthropy/youthvoices/.

Bay Area Video Coalition/YouthLINK. (2006). Retrieved June 7, 2007, from http://www.bavc.org/nextgen/youthlink/index.html.

Bridges to Understanding. (2005). Retrieved June 7, 2007, from http://www. bridgesweb.org/.

British Broadcasting Corporation. (June 7, 2007). *Capture Wales.* Retrieved June 7, 2007, from http://www.bbc.co.uk/wales/capturewales/.

Center for Digital Storytelling. (n.d.). Retrieved June 7, 2007, from http://www.storycenter.org.

Eduweave. (2007). Retrieved June 7, 2007, from http://www.eduweave.org/.

Home Depot True Stories. (2007). Retrieved June 7, 2007, from http://www6. homedepot.com/truestories/.

I-10Witness Program. (n.d.). Retrieved June 7, 2007, from http://i10witness. org/.

Lambert, J. (2002). *Digital storytelling: Capturing lives, creating community.* Berkeley, CA: Digital Diner Press.

———. (January 13, 2006). *Incorporating digital storytelling into teaching and learning.* Lecture presented at the University of Maryland–Baltimore County, Baltimore, MD. Retrieved June 7, 2007, from http://asp1. umbc.edu/newmedia/studio/stream/qtdetail.cfm?recordID=388.

Marcuss, M. (2007). The new community anthology: Digital storytelling as a community development strategy. *c&b,* 9–13. Retrieved June 7, 2007, from www.creativenarrations.net/digital.pdf.

National Public Radio. (n.d.). *StoryCorps.* Retrieved June 7, 2007, from http:// storycorps.net/.

———. (n.d.) *StoryCorps. Griot Initiative.* Retrieved June 7, 2007, from http:// www.storycorps.net/griot.

Rooney, B. (June 2, 2007). Welcome to "Cellywood": Movies hit the tiny screen. *ABC News.* Retrieved June 2, 2007, from http://abcnews.go. com/print?id=3140596.

Silence Speaks. (n.d.). Retrieved June 7, 2007, from http://www. silencespeaks.org/.

Stories for Change. (n.d.). Retrieved June 7, 2007, from http:// storiesforchange.net/about_stories_for_change.

Storybuilders. (n.d.). Retrieved June 7, 2007, from http://www. storybuilders.org/.

StoryMapping. (n.d.). Retrieved June 7, 2007, from http://www. storymapping.org/.

Tharp, K. W. and Hills, L. (2004). Digital storytelling: Culture, media and community. In S. Marshall, W. Taylor, and X. Yu (Eds.), *Using Community informatics to transform regions* (pp. 37–51). Hershey, PA: Idea Group Publishing.

Thomson-Gale. (n.d.). *Librareo*. Retrieved http://www.gale.com/librareo/.

University of California–Berkeley, Social Technologies Group. (2007). *Street stories*. Retrieved June 7, 2007, from http://www2.sims.berkeley.edu/research/projects/socialtech/.

CHAPTER 3
Social Networking and Its Relationship to Digital Storytelling

SOCIAL NETWORKING BUILDS COMMUNITY

The academic library has arrived at a particularly propitious moment to tell stories and tell them digitally. Our students are pointing the way for us. Every day we see them using multimodal and Web 2.0 technologies to build community among themselves through social networking sites. The catastrophic events of September 11, 2001, may not have brought social networking into being, but it is difficult to imagine that they have not accelerated the growth in the number of social networking venues and the extent of their use for community-building. Suddenly the world looks bigger, more dangerous, and lonelier than it did before, and we have learned to treasure our connections to one another. Social networking helps create and strengthen those connections.

Social networks are Web sites and Web-based applications that enable users to communicate among themselves. Sometimes these users know each other in real life; sometimes they meet, virtually, as strangers. Social networking sites cast webs of community, however, and soon their users are no longer strangers. From something as simple as an instant messaging buddy list grows a whole network of acquaintances and friends. Every week, opening the technology sections in the popular press reveals a new genre or a new twist on an existing genre. Between the writing of this book and its publication it is difficult to predict which virtual social networks will still be thriving and which will have been superseded by new ones. It seems safe to predict, however, that the use of social networking as a means of establishing, growing, and maintaining community is a trend that will be around for a long time, particularly among the young people who are the primary populations of U.S. colleges and universities in the early twenty-first century, the so-called Millenials.

Millenials, those born since 1982, are described by Oblinger as young people whose "learning preferences tend toward teamwork, experiential activities, structure, and the use of technology. Their strengths include multitasking, goal orientation, positive attitudes, and a collaborative style" (Oblinger 2003, 38). Their team-oriented attitude, ability to multitask, and comfort with technology make them ripe for social networking. The discomfort that their elders might feel in welcoming friends from virtually anywhere without any kind of real filters or social preliminaries seems not to threaten this generation. "Reality is no longer real. Those things that appear real over the Internet may not be. Digital images may have been altered. E-mail sent from someone's address may not have come from that person. And the content may or may not be accurate" (Oblinger 2003, 38). The new reality for Millenials is the social reality they construct through the use of new technologies.

New communication technologies such as online chat, instant messaging, text messaging, and voice-over-IP have made Millenials comfortable with non–face-to-face environments. Mobile technology devices such as cell phones, smart phones, iPods, and VideoPods have enabled them to carry social networks with them wherever they go.

MySpace, FaceBook, and their predecessors *Classmates.com* and *Friendster* have encouraged young people to put their faces, their thoughts, and their "favorites" out in front of the world. Users browse these sites, lurking on the networks of those with similar affinities, for instance, political issues, comic books, and fraternities and sororities. Eventually, they may post a comment, a photo, or a video until ultimately they feel themselves a member of that network, that community. A recent check of the four thousand-member *FaceBook* network for my *alma mater,* a women's college, revealed students rallying together to sign a petition to stop the forced retirement of the golf coach. They were also reassuring an incoming first year student that there indeed would be a social life that includes men, and they were hailing an alumna who not only designed the original icons for Apple computers but is now creating *"Facebook* gifts," clever icons that can be attached to a friend's *Facebook* entry in return for a donation to breast cancer research.

A variation on *MySpace* and *Facebook* is *Twitter*, a site that describes itself as "a global community of friends and strangers answering one simple question: 'What are you doing?'" Lest this sound like a total waste of time both for the twitterers and the twitterees, Jason Pontin (2007) argues, "Sending tweets broadcasts, 'I am alive!' Reading tweets satisfies the craving of many people to know the smallest details of the lives of those they love," voices of brothers, sisters, and friends whose instant messages and phone calls otherwise may skimp on such details.

Wikis are a kind of social network too. Characterized by their goal of organizing information in a collaborative manner, wikis by their nature invite users to interact by editing content. *Wikipedia*, started in 2001, is probably the most well-known wiki, designed to be an online encyclopedia to which readers contribute entries and which all readers, unless they have abused their privileges on the site, are free to edit.

From *Wikocracy*, which allows users to rewrite laws and court decisions and generally transform the U.S. legal system, to *Wookieepedia*, which caters to *Star Wars* fans, most wikis share information rather than stories. One, though—*A Million Penguins* (Penguin 2007)—is a collaborative novel in progress. Many businesses and professional organizations, including libraries, now use wiki technology to share and organize information. Libraries, for instance, can have a reference section on which staff and even student assistants can update information about current class assignments that are sending students to the reference desk, new databases, and answers to challenging questions. Our library wiki has a section on grant opportunities that directs librarians to a variety of resources and tips useful for applying for and obtaining grants.

Blogs, short for "Weblogs," consist of millions of stories told by their creators. The original purpose of a blog was to enable an individual to share personal online journal entries with the world. Today bloggers send personal thoughts, experiences, and stories out into the world, never sure who if anyone is reading them. Blogs give their writers opportunity for creative and expressive release. They also have a threading response capability, so blogs have evolved into a two-way, three-way, essentially unlimited way for people to communicate with one another, potentially providing the dynamic, triangular relationship among teller, tale, and audience.

Checking the blog directories offered by *Technorati* and *Google Blogsearch* reveals blogs with everything from provocative but respectable news punditry by Arianna Huffington (Huffington 2007) to celebrity gossip at *Access Hollywood. Outside.in* will detect the location of your computer and provide access to blogs from your local neighborhood. Bloggers can add links to news stories, restaurant Web sites, and other sites of interest to others in their neighborhood. Did you know that Harlem is the eighth "bloggiest" neighborhood in the United States?

Ning invites users to "create your own social network," for instance, *PezHeads* for collectors of Pez candy dispensers. *CrowdVine* and *Live-Journal* are two of many others that resemble *Ning* in their goal of joining together people of every stripe.

The 2004 presidential campaign of Howard Dean used a blog in a way original at that time to raise money in a singularly populist manner without the intervention of political action committees and high-dollar fundraising events. From there, blogging has continued its spread into the political arena. During the 2004 presidential nominating conventions and on the 2006 congressional election night, network and cable news networks shared their platforms with bloggers such as Michele Catalano of *The Command Post*. In 2007, Joshua Micah Marshall's *Talking Points Memo* blog played a key role in stirring popular interest in and subsequent response on Capitol Hill to the U.S. Attorneys firing scandal. Even the United Nations has granted press credentials to a blogger not affiliated with a large media organization, Matthew Lee. As we navigate the 2008 presidential campaign it is clear that blogs and the networks they have spawned among all kinds of people with access to the Internet have broadened access to the political process.

Multimedia applications have enabled sharing of video, still image, and audio files. *YouTube*, perhaps the best known, provides a site where users can post film and video created by themselves and by others. *Flikr* and *Photobucket* are examples of photo sharing sites that include features for blogging, comment-sharing, and posting information about the photographers. *Photobucket* has teamed with *CherryTap*, which describes itself as an "online pub and happy hour," a convivial place for strangers, as well as friends. *iTunes* not only serves as an agent for download and purchase of popular music, but it allows users to trade their own musical compositions and audio podcasts.

One step beyond a blog is a vlog, or a video blog, a blog that includes video. *Alive in Baghdad* (Conley 2007) was created by a group of American and Iraqi news correspondents to show the events in Iraq from a different point of view than might be seen in western television news accounts. Even *Al Quaeda* has a unit called *Al Sahab* (*The Cloud*), Naim (2007) points out, whose goal is to attract major media attention to their videos. *Mog* offers mogs, blogs with music, as well as *YouTube* videos.

With *Kyte* social networking has gone mobile. Users can download *Kyte* software to their cell phones and broadcast pictures and videos on personal *Kyte* channels, providing open access to anyone who is interested in being informed of every immediate detail of the *Kyte* broadcasters' lives. *Tiny Pictures* uses *Radar* software as does *Kyte*, although you must be invited to view member pictures.

A subcategory of social networking, or perhaps one means of social networking, is social bookmarking, or folksonomies. Based on Vannevar Bush's pioneering concept that "associative trails" (Bush 1945, para. 63) could provide access to information and move beyond the limitations of indexing, social bookmarking allows users to tag favorites— be they blogs, songs, videos, books, or virtually anything else. Social bookmarking sites link people with similar tags into virtual communities by virtue of the choices they have indicated. *de.li.cio.us* is one such example. Primarily designed as a site for storing and organizing one's personal online bookmarks, its mobility features (it can be used on any computer from any location) makes it a much more flexible system than one tied to the desktop. Once one's personal bookmarks are stored and organized they can be shared among fellow *de.li.cio.us* members, who can search for members with similar interests. As the *de.li.cio.us* Web site claims, "Everyone on *de.li.cio.us* chooses to save their bookmarks for a reason." The discovered links between those reasons for saving bookmarks builds community. Similar to *de.li.cio.us* are *MyStrands*, *UpTo11*, *Last.fm*, and *Librarything.com*.

As if born swimming in this world, Millenials also feel comfortable in whole virtual worlds, such as the one growing on *Second Life*. Since 2003, 5,618,501 residents have established personal avatars in *Second Life*. Clubs, libraries, games, gallery openings, and even whole college campuses are examples of places and events to be found there. The introductory screens offer a somewhat eerie welcome: "Within your first hour, you'll notice that several residents approach you and introduce themselves—*Second Lifers* are eager to welcome you and show you around. Within this vibrant society of people, it's easy to find people with similar interests to you. Once you meet people you like, you find it's easy to communicate and stay in touch. At any time there are dozens of events where you can party at nightclubs, attend fashion shows and art openings, or just play games. Residents also form groups ranging from neighborhood associations to fans of sci fi movies."

The role of social networking, as well as mobile communication technology, in the lives of Millenials was no more dramatically displayed than on the day of the horrific shootings at Virginia Polytechnic Institute in April, 2007 and the days immediately following. A video captured on a student's cell phone was played again and again on commercial television, as well as *YouTube*, bringing to the world the sound of gunshots echoing from Norris Hall in real time. Cell phone calls were made to reassure parents and friends and, in turn, to seek reassurance. Virginia Tech students communicated that day via their *FaceBook* pages, warning friends not to go near campus, calling out for responses from missing classmates, and—finally—posting memorial messages when they learned those messages would never be returned. When the videos left behind by the shooter were discovered soon after the murders, they were played only briefly on national news for fear of glorifying the killer or inspiring copycat acts, but the videos live on in the world of *YouTube*, even alongside parody videos. The disturbing play scripts that alerted students to their classmate's violent potential were promptly posted online to a *Wikipedia* entry, underscoring the power of social networking sites to make every person a journalist in his own right.

The professional news media combed *FaceBook* pages for contacts with students. Students were finally so overwhelmed by the intrusion into their community that they begged the news media to get out of their pages. Certainly students had posed the same requests in person, but the movement from face-to-face confrontation into the virtual world demonstrates how powerful a tool these social networking sites have become not only for building bridges within a community, but for closing off those bridges to those seen as outsiders during the most stressful times.

SOCIAL NETWORKING AND DIGITAL STORYTELLING

Many, if not most, *YouTube* videos are frivolous, *ad hoc* cell phone captures of little interest to anyone other than their creators. They appear to have been created in total social isolation and just tossed like water balloons from the top of a tall building with little concern for whom they might hit. Fortunately, though, a significant number of *YouTube* videos have at least the potential to be fully fledged digital stories, showing evidence of all seven elements mentioned by Lambert: "point (of view), dramatic question, emotional content, gift of your voice, power of the soundtrack, economy, [and] pacing" (Lambert 2002, xi).

Schwartzberg's (2006) *YAC-The Bike Messenger* is an excellent example of a video with all seven elements. The dramatic question could either be, why does he risk his life daily in this enterprise or, will he make it through this particular day in one piece. Schwartzberg allows YAC to narrate the video himself, adding a genuine New York street flavor to this day-in-the-life story. Music is used sparingly but effectively, and pacing alternates between thrilling views from YAC's vantage point careening through the streets of Manhattan and interludes of relative quiet as he waits for elevators or catches quick bites to eat. Weinshenker's (2006) ironically titled *Grand Canyons* is a quieter example that reflects on his parents' divorce.

Some videos created in a digital storytelling setting are posted on *YouTube* and even tagged as digital stories. For example, Marie Caso's (2005) *Woman in Black Boots*, created with television station CCTV in Cambridge, Massachusetts through their *Computers for Elders* program, is there, as is Jack Nguyen's (2006) story about teens and domestic violence created in conjunction with the Dorchester, Massachusetts *Close to Home Domestic Violence Prevention Initiative*. Some are created in school and college classrooms such as Chris Engler's (2007) and Michelle Sabourin's (2006) respectively.

Perhaps these social networking technologies have not provided as much community as we might expect, however. A 2007 study by Hitwise (Auchard 2007), a company that measures Web audiences, reported that only 0.0016 percent of *YouTube* users actually uploaded videos. The rest visited to watch what others had posted. Users of *Flickr* who actually posted photos represented only 0.002 percent. *Wikipedia* contributers weighed in at 4.6 percent. Wood may have offered a cynical explanation: "Visiting most social networking sites is akin to getting invited to a party where all the cool kids are going, then showing up and finding out there's no food, no drinks, no band, no games, no pool, nothing. Just a bunch of painful small talk and leering grins. The people-watching can hold your interest for only so long" (Wood 2005, para. 5).

In a 2007 presentation on information overload, Levy characterized personal information overload as a function of quantity of information, time, and the need to pay attention, all at an increasingly accelerating speed. (The phrase *viral video*, coined to describe the spread of videos through the Web by means of sites like *YouTube*, conveys well this sense of pandemic.) Levy compared this "environmental crisis" of the spirit to something on the scale of global warming. Speaking of technology in general, he posited that instead of signifying a search for connection with others, our increasing absorption in technology may indicate a lack of comfort with being alone with oneself. Levy's description brings to mind Julie Christie's character, Mildred Montag, in *Fahrenheit 451*, a housewife reduced to endlessly staring at the television screen in a society that forbids books.

Nevertheless, both Heffernan and Lambert agree that the situation is not so bleak and that social networking sites can provide a healthy environment for developing community through digital storytelling. In Heffernan's view, the text can completely disappear in a video-based environment: "Really the only authentic response to a *YouTube* video is another *YouTube* video—the so-called 'video response,'" a feature of the *YouTube* site that invites users to post responses in video format. "In answer to a lousy stammering video, say, a real YouTuber doesn't just comment, 'You idiot—I could do that blindfolded!' He blindfolds himself, gets out his video-capable Canon PowerShot and uploads the results" (Heffernan 2007, 1). Far from being a negative thing, videos and their video responses are resulting in a burgeoning number of online minicommunities, Heffernan claims. One such *YouTube* community has grown out of senior citizens responding with their own video oral histories to the vlog of Peter Oakley, *Peter Oakley, aka Geriatric 1927*, a British retiree. Another *YouTube* community has grown up around Joy Nash's *Fat Rant*, a proclamation of pride in her 224-pound weight.

Lambert's view is more text-oriented, but no less optimistic: "In our work, we use the visual culture to bring people back into language and the written word. Many educators see our approach as a critical tool for increasing the quality and thoughtfulness of writing. I think writing into the screen is a natural place for people to go, from *Flickr* image stories, to digital stories, to writing dialogue and narrations for fictional and documentary films. People will see the way text skills improve these modes of visual communication. The notion of collaboration in creating narrative becomes much more interesting with the ubiquity of online networks. Undoubtedly, the way people share stories and respond, either in text on a blog or in trading stories as videos on *YouTube*, creates enormously fluid and generative mechanisms for story" (Lambert 2007, para. 1).

The key to making room in a social networking environment for digital storytelling is to find ways to stimulate people not just to be passive consumers of the enormous amount of content available on social networking sites, but to be active producers not just of content but of meaningful content. This means that they have planned, selected, molded, and revised their ideas into forms that can engage their audience, whether that audience is sitting in the same room with them or out in cyberspace. The socially based programs of storytelling that we have already described and the academically based programs that we will describe all can give people the skills, trust, and confidence they need to begin connecting on the Web through storytelling.

REFERENCES

Access Hollywood. (n.d.). *Access blogs.* Retrieved June 4, 2007, from http://blogs.accesshollywood.com/.

Auchard, Eric. *Participation on Web 2.0 sites remains weak.* Retrieved May 19, 2007, from http://www.reuters.com/articlePrint?articleId=USN1743638820070418.

Bush, Vannevar. As we may think. *The Atlantic Monthly,* July 1945. Retrieved May 18, 2007, from *The Atlantic Online,* http://www.theatlantic.com/doc/print/194507/bush.

Caso, Marie (Writer and Producer). (2005). *Woman in black boots.* Retrieved June 5, 2007, from http://www.youtube.com/watch?v=Y1m93kprVvs.

Catalano, Michele. (2007). *The command post.* Retrieved June 4, 2007, from http://www.command-post.org/.

CherryTap. (2007). Retrieved June 4, 2007, from http://www.cherrytap.com/.

Classmates.com. (2007). Retrieve June 4, 2007, from http://www.classmates.com.

Conley, Brian. (June 4, 2007). *Alive in Baghdad.* Retrieved June 4, 2007, from http://aliveinbaghdad.org/.

CrowdVine. (2007). Retrieved June 4, 2007, from http://www.crowdvine.com/home.

de.li.cio.us. (2007). Retrieved June 4, 2007, from http://de.li.cio.us.com.

Engler, Chris (Writer and Producer). (April 17, 2007). *Cozad basketball digital story.* Retrieved June 5, 2007, from http://www.youtube.com/watch?v=LEoTKxr9EyY.

FaceBook. (2007). Retrieved June 4, 2007, from http://www.facebook.com.

Flickr. (2007). Retrieved June 4, 2007, from http://www.flickr.com.

Friendster. (2007). Retrieved June 4, 2007, from http://www.friendster.com.

Google Blogsearch. (2007). Retrieved June 4, 2007, from http://blogsearch.google.com.

Heffernan, Virginia. (May 27, 2007). The many tribes of YouTube. *The New York Times,* p. 2, 23.

Huffington, Arianna. (June 4, 2007). *The Huffington post.* Retrieved June 4, 2007, from http://www.huffingtonpost.com.

iTunes. (2007). Retrieved June 4, 2007, from http://www.itunes.com.

Kyte. (2007). Retrieved June 4, 2007, from http://www.kyte.tv.

Lambert, Joe. (2007). Digital storytelling [electronic version]. *Futurist,* 41, 25.

Last.fm. (2007). Retrieved June 4, 2007, from http://www.last.fm.

Lee, Matthew Russell. (June 3, 2007). *Inner City Press at the UN.* Retrieved June 4, 2007, from http://innercitypress.com.

Levy, David. (May 22, 2007). *Information overload.* Lecture presented at The Ohio State University, Columbus, OH.

LibraryThing.com. (2007). Retrieved June 4, 2007, from http://www.librarything.com.

LiveJournal. (2007). Retrieved June 4, 2007, from http://www.livejournal.com/.

Marshall, Joshua Micah. (June 4, 2007). *Talking points memo.* Retrieved June 4, 2007, from http://www.talkingpointsmemo.com/.

Mog. (2007). Retrieved June 4, 2007, from http://www.mog.com.

MySpace. (2007). Retrieved June 4, 2007, from http://www.myspace.com.

MyStrands. (2007). Retrieved June 4, 2007, from http://www.mystrands.com.

Naim, Moises. (January/February 2007). The YouTube effect: How a technology for teenagers became a force for political and economic change [electronic version]. *Foreign Policy,* 104–103 [sic].

Nguyen, Jack. (Writer and Producer). (June 26, 2006). *Digital storytelling.* Retrieved June 5, 2007, from http://www.youtube.com/watch?v=EVphlKJy6Yc.

Ning. (2007). Retrieved June 4, 2007, from http://www.ning.com/.

Oblinger, Diana (July/August 2003). Boomers, Gen-Xers, and Millenials: Understanding the new students [electronic version]. *Educause Review,* 37–39.

Outside.in. (2007). Retrieved June 4, 2007, from http://outside.in/.

————. (2007). *Bloggiest neighborhoods.* Retrieved June 4, 2007, from http://outside.in/news/bloggiest_neighborhoods.php.

Penguin Books and De Montfort University. (March 7, 2007). *A million penguins.* Retrieved June 4, 2007, from http://www.amillionpenguins.com/.

Photobucket. (2007). Retrieved June 4, 2007, from http://photobucket.com/.

Pontin, Jason. (April 22, 2007). Slipstream: From many tweets, one loud voice on the Internet. *New York Times,* p. BU3.

Sabourin, Michelle (Writer and Producer). (December 12, 2006). *Who am I?* Retrieved June 5, 2007, from http://www.youtube.com/watch?v=LEoTKxr9EyY.

Schwartzberg, Louis (Producer). (2006). *YAC-New York bike messenger.* Retrieved June 5, 2007, from http://www.youtube.com/watch?v=sj1-218EnvY.

Second Life. (2007). Retrieved June 4, 2007, from http://secondlife.com.

Technorati. (2007). Retrieved June 4, 2007, from http://technorati.com.

Tiny Pictures. (2007). Retrieved June 4, 2007, from http://www.tinypictures. us/radar.html.

Twitter. (2007). Retrieved June 4, 2007, from http://twitter.com.

UpTo11. (2007). Retrieved June 4, 2007, from http://www.upto11.net.

Weinshenker, Daniel (Writer and Producer). (December 13, 2006). *Grand canyons*. Retrieved June 5, 2007, from http://www.youtube.com/ watch?v=LEoTKxr9EyY.

Wikipedia. (June 2, 2007). Retrieved June 4, 2007, from http://www. wikipedia.com.

Wikocracy. (March 16, 2006). Retrieved June 4, 2007, from http://www. wikocracy.com/.

Wood, Molly. (June 2, 2005). *The buzz report: Five reasons social networking doesn't work*. Retrieved June 4, 2007, from *cnet.com*, http://www. cnet.com/4520-6033_1-6240550-1.html.

Wookieepedia. (2005). Retrieved June 4, 2007, from http://starwars.wikia. com/wiki/Main_Page.

YouTube. (2007). Retrieved June 4, 2007, from http://www.youtube.com.

CHAPTER 4
Social Technologies, Stories, and Higher Education

Every year for the last four years, the New Media Consortium (2007) has published *The Horizon Report*. It scans technologies and higher education to see what likely will be impacting academia for the next year, the next two to three years, and what might be on the horizon in the next three to five years. The 2007 report indicates that the immediate technologies higher education faces are user-created content and social technologies. When we consider that many students blog, vlog, research with *Wikipedia*, have *Facebook* or *MySpace* pages, watch the latest viral video on *YouTube* (or maybe submit it themselves) and share pictures through online services such as *Flickr*, the conclusions of the report are not at all surprising.

In describing user created-content, *The Horizon Report* indicates, "It's all about the audience, and the 'audience' is no longer merely listening" (New Media Consortium 2007, para. 4). In their personal lives, students are not passively surfing the Web any longer. They are helping to create it, they are buying and selling on it, and they are downloading entertainment from it. Students do not consider the Web a technology any more than they consider the electricity required to run it a technology. The Web is quickly becoming a way of life. Thus it makes sense that it is an important piece of students' social fabric.

The challenge then for higher education is finding ways to harness these technology trends to improve and enhance student learning. *The Horizon Report* further indicates that "[s]ocial networking may represent a key way to increase student access to and participation in course activities. It is more than just a friends list; truly engaging social networking offers an opportunity to contribute, share, communicate, and collaborate" (New Media Consortium 2007, para. 5). Academia can guide students toward contributing more meaningful dialog and content to the social network, and thus to society.

PEDAGOGIES

An interesting convergence of learning theories with technologies has been evolving for some time now. In a seminal article by Barr and Tagg, we see learning institutions moving from an "Instruction Paradigm" to a "Learning Paradigm" in which "learning environments and activities are learner-centered and learner-controlled" (Barr and Tagg 1995, *Learning Theory* section, para. 3). Such a paradigm rejects the notion of learner as a vessel and instead requires action and involvement on the part of the learner.

This has caused a shift from purely lecture-based classes to increased incorporation of active learning techniques. In active learning, the instructor seeks to engage the student in learning by doing, rather than pure lecture. Increasingly instructors are seeing the value of discovery-based learning, where the student has to work toward an answer in contrast to the method of assuming students will absorb every piece of content that can be crammed into a lecture. Today, the advocacy for active learning strategies is coming just when these strategies can be buoyed by new technologies.

Happily, Web 2.0 applications and other new technologies are providing new and interesting ways for students to rise to the occasion and contribute content to classes in ways previously not possible. Increasingly students can participate in content creation, content sharing, and in responding to each other in new ways. Learners no longer just passively soak up knowledge.

Additionally, students are learning to use new technologies in lower and lower grades as new software becomes increasingly accessible both in cost and ease of use. The U.S. Department of Education reported that in 2003 "about 91 percent (53 million persons) of children age 3 and over and in nursery school through grade 12 use computers, and about 59 percent (35 million persons) use the Internet" (DeBell and Chapman 2006, iii). While this statistic does not guarantee that students in K-12 all are receiving active learning education, it does indicate that students are increasingly used to hands-on activities that involve technology. Students heading toward college will expect some of this same sort of hands-on technology to be part of their education.

Another trend in higher education is a broadening of literacy studies to include an examination of literacy within cultural contexts, thus introducing the notion of multiple literacies (Street 2003). Multiple literacies are becoming important both due to our increasingly multicultural society and new technology. Some of the literacies being explored and taught include print, media (television, radio, Internet), multimedia (visual, audio, film), and computer literacy. And because of our global and multicultural environment, added to these are social and cultural literacies.

Michael Wesch (2007), a cultural anthropologist at Kansas State University, received attention when his video *Web 2.0 . . . The Machine Is Us/ing Us* about how malleable text, and consequently information, is in the Web environment received millions of hits on *YouTube*. This fame has exposed some extended work he is doing with classes using vlogging (video blogging) and examining the ethnography of online communities (Young 2007). Wesch's work truly blends multimedia and the culturally expanded notion of multiple literacies.

Media literacy is a complex literacy, actually encompassing many others. It is an especially important one to highlight in the discussion of storytelling, as storytelling is one component of this literacy.

"Media literacy" involves knowledge of how media work, how they construct meaning, how they serve as a form of cultural pedagogy, and how they function in everyday life . . . The media are both crucial sources of knowledge and information, and sources of entertainment and leisure activity. They are our storytellers and entertainers, and are especially influential since we are often not aware that media narratives and spectacles themselves are a form of education, imparting cultural knowledge, values, and shaping how we see and live our social worlds . . . Media literacy thus requires traditional print literacy skills as well as visual literacy, aural literacy, and the ability to analyze narratives, spectacles, and a wide range of cultural forms . . . Thus, on this conception, genuine computer literacy involves not just technical knowledge and skills, but refined reading, writing, and communicating ability that involves heightened capacities for critically analyzing, interpreting, and processing print, image, sound, and multimedia material. Computer literacy involves intensified abilities to read, to scan texts and information, to put together in meaningful patterns mosaics of information, to construct meanings and significance, to contextualize and evaluate, and to discuss and articulate one's own views. (Kellner 1998, *New Technologies, Multiple Literacies, and Postmodern Pedagogy: The New Frontier* section, para. 2)

This definition of media literacy mentions visual literacy, another literacy also attracting attention in academia. Visual literacy includes the ability to receive and interpret visual information and to express oneself visually. For instance, taking an historical event and portraying it graphically as a timeline, or taking numerical data and constructing interesting and meaningful charts with various representations would exemplify visual literacy. Visual literacy is not necessarily new, but as with so many areas of education, visual literacy is being both challenged and aided by new technologies. Often the types of classroom activities that might be mentioned in conjunction with developing visual literacy might include: creating PowerPoint presentations, using single images as prompts for creative writing, building presentations with images but without text, evaluating authenticity of visual information, virtual field trips using *Flickr*, reading maps, and evaluating spatial information using *Google Earth*. Also included in this category might be digital storytelling.

STORY

But digital storytelling requires more than visual literacy and technology skills. It also requires the ability to tell a story and learn from stories. While the *2007 Horizon Report* highlights user-created content, including digital stories, as an imminent technology, and even though some schools are already adopting this technology, the report also notes: "There is a skills gap between understanding how to use tools for media creation and how to create meaningful content. Although new tools make it increasingly easy to produce multimedia works, students lack essential skills in composition, storytelling, and design" (New Media Consortium, Critical Challenges, 2007, para. 5).

Thus it is important to note that while it is easy to assume most students have the skills to make a digital story, in fact there are many components needed to create meaningful stories and it is unlikely that most students are well-versed in all these areas. While digital storytelling can be an excellent presentation technique for both teaching and learning, it still needs to be taught.

In fact, English departments are expanding the notion of composition to move beyond pen-and-paper and word processor to multimodal composition. Multimodal composition can include audio, still visual, and video expression. For instance, a composition class might now teach and require students to compose an audio piece that first includes textual scriptwriting to create the story, but then also the technical skills to record the writer's voice reading the script, the ability to choose and add an appropriate soundtrack, and technical skills to affect the recording quality (perhaps a crisper effect, an echo, or a scratched and aged effect) to make the piece richer and more meaningful.

In their literature review McDrury and Alterio (2003) thoroughly document how essential the notion of reflection is to the learning process and how storytelling supports reflection. The learning theorists they investigate relate the importance of reflection to deep learning. Reflection allows feelings and emotions to become part of the learning process and allows learners to contextualize what they are learning. Stories help incorporate emotion often lacking in more formal cognitive education. Contextualization comes when we examine events in a story in light of our known cultural context compared to unexpected or new ideas presented in the story. As we seek to understand the new, we mediate between that and the known world.

Consider also how important stories are in lectures. It is often through stories that the successful lecturer connects with students and generates interest. Engaging lecturers infuse story, humor, examples, and a variety of other techniques to hold student interest and make the topic relevant.

Storytelling in community allows students to engage in dialogue centered on the story. "Through dialogue, shaped to explore experiences in depth, multiple perspectives can emerge. From these perspectives, new learning and relationships can be constructed" (McDrury and Alterio 2003, 39). This highlights the importance of building community or working in groups when using storytelling for learning in an academic setting. Further, it makes the case that storytelling in formal settings produces more learning than storytelling in informal settings. Dinner table or coffee break storytelling is "hijacked" (McDrury and Alterio 2003, 52) by similar stories from participants that may steer the conversation in a different way. In a formal setting, storytellers are afforded an audience responsive to their stories and to their questions about their stories. This is precisely how the story circle functions in a digital storytelling workshop.

Beyond the theory and scholarship of the usefulness of stories, the application of story into pedagogical practice is not so new to higher education. But just as with other trends in education, technology is highlighting story in new ways. Consider other teaching methods that have been used for some time now. In many respects, the case study method has always been about putting the learner into the middle of a story, letting him perform as an actor in the story and influence its outcome. Students must confront villains and overcome obstacles. This has been a standard means of instruction in business schools, most notably the Harvard Business School. The case method also is well-established in schools of law and medicine.

The University of Buffalo has established a Center for Case Study Teaching in Science, taking the principles and ideas from business, medicine, and law and is applying these into a science framework. In various columns written for scientists to learn how to write case studies, Herreid (1998) lists a variety of elements that are contained in a good case study, some of which overlap with Lambert's (2002) seven elements of a good digital story. The point of a story or a case is what makes it relevant, generalizable to a wide audience, and of enduring importance. Point of view helps to create first an emotional connection and then empathy between the speaker and the audience involved in the problem. Sometimes this includes use of the first person perspective and dialogue, or what Herreid calls "quotations" (Herreid 1998, para. 9).

Also of key importance is the notion of the dramatic question. The dramatic question wins learners' attention, makes them think, and makes them care. By struggling with the dramatic question students learn, fulfilling the pedagogic goals of the case method. Finally, economy, or brevity, is important to both case and story. One pedagogic reason for this is to turn grappling with the question or problem over to the learners. If too much time is spent on the case or on the story, the learners do not have sufficient time to consider the issues on their own or even sufficient ambiguity over which to ponder.

The notion of point in stories and case method relates back again to Barr and Tagg (1995) who state that in a learning paradigm students must learn within a framework. It is not enough to have students memorize disparate facts and processes that seem to apply only to the course at hand. In a learning environment students understand the broader framework within which the facts and processes are valid. The generalizability or universality of a case or a story provides this framework, thus providing meaning.

A method of teaching related to active learning that many disciplines are adopting is problem-based learning (PBL). With PBL students working in collaborative groups are given a real world, open-ended problem to solve. They are given insufficient information to solve the problem and so must find that information. The solution generally requires research, analysis, and collaboration. The instructor acts as a guide, or helper. As with the case method, "problem-based learning . . . ends up orienting students toward meaning-making over fact-collecting. They learn via contextualized problem sets and situations"

Table 4.1 The Seven Elements, Case Method, and PBL Compared

Seven Elements (Lambert 2002)	Case Method (Herreid 1998)	PBL (Duch 1996)
	Tells a story	
Dramatic question	Focuses on an interest-arousing issue; has pedagogic utility; provokes conflict	Engaging, real-world; students have a stake; should relate to the course goals; requires students to make decisions or judgments
	Is set in the past five years	
Point of view; emotional content	Creates empathy with the central characters	
Point of view; gift of your voice	Includes quotations	
Point	Is relevant to the reader; is generalizable	Has one or more of the following: open-ended, not limited to one correct answer; connected to previously learned knowledge; controversial issues that will elicit diverse opinions
Economy	Is short	Length and complexity of problems should be controlled to force cooperation, not divide and conquer.

(Rhem 1998, para. 2). What might distinguish PBL from storytelling is that PBL is all about solving problems, whereas stories act more to create the environment for discussing problems and learning, not necessarily learning directed at solving a specific problem. What the two do have in common is the general sense of context and meaning-making.

Story is an inherent part of PBL because of the engagement, empathy, and context that must be present in successful and meaningful PBL.

Lest we overstate the connections among digital storytelling, the case study method, and PBL, we must acknowledge that these are all distinct activities with varying goals and outcomes. But they do have common themes, making it possible to see how digital storytelling can contribute to learning in much the same way as the case method and PBL do because of their use of story.

One further development related to stories in higher education is the use of electronic portfolios. Barrett has begun linking digital storytelling to the creation of electronic portfolios and considers the resulting product to be a "reflective portfolio" (Barrett 2004, para.1) that is learner-centered and goes beyond institutional necessities of assessment.

Another analysis of the pedagogy of story in the learning process is Egan's (1988) work on storytelling as a framework for teaching itself. Egan directs his efforts toward curriculum development for children. Table 4.2 compares his curricular ideas, pedagogies used in higher education, and the elements of digital storytelling. It is easy to see how Tables 4.1 and 4.2 could be further collapsed to show common elements among all these theories built around story, and how in fact these elements are all related to the seven elements of digital storytelling defined by Lambert (2002).

One important story-related idea of Egan's (1988) that is not represented in Table 4.2 is the importance of imagination in education. Egan describes imagination as an important tool children use to mediate between nature and culture and that is often neglected in formal education. Through imagination, children learn to move between what is scientifically true and what is culturally true. This is the same type of mediation, like between hot and cold, that is used to navigate between life and death through such imaginary concepts as spirits and ghosts. Imagination helps fuel the human ability to deal with complexity beyond a computer-like use of our brains. This sense of imagination that we were wired with as children can continue to teach us to make these navigations between scientific fact and cultural reality even as adults.

The importance of imagination in the educational structure envisioned by Egan harkens back to Pink's (2005) claims that we are more than just left-brained, computer-like processors. The more holistic right-brained characteristics of "subjectivity, intuition, and synthesizing" help us with this navigation between science and culture as well. And as both Pink and Egan believe, story is one important tool for

Table 4.2 Seven Elements and Curriculum Development

Seven Elements (Lambert 2002)	Curriculum Development (Egan 1988)
Point	Identifying importance: What is most important about this topic? Why should it matter to [children] my audience? What is affectively engaging about it?
Dramatic question	Finding binary opposites: What binary opposites best catch the importance of the topic?
Point of view, emotion, soundtrack, pacing, gift of your voice	Organizing content into story form What content most dramatically embodies the binary opposites, in order to provide access to the topic? What content best articulates the topic into a developing story form? Among these grasping or grappling tools are the ability to make sense of things in terms of human intentions, emotions, hopes, fears, etc. By personalizing the impersonal we can use these tools.
Point	Conclusion What is the best way of resolving the dramatic conflict inherent in the binary opposites? What degree of mediation of those opposites is it appropriate to seek? Evaluation How can one know whether the topic has been understood, its importance grasped, and the content learned?

navigation between these two realities and between these two sides of our brains.

Egan's assertions complement Bruner's advocacy of folk psychology. In *Acts of Meaning*, he makes the case that folk psychology should not be subservient to scientific psychology because culture, not biology makes our actions meaningful. He states: "[O]ur capacity to render experience in terms of narrative is not just child's play, but an instrument for making meaning that dominates much of life in culture—from soliloquies at bedtime to the weighing of testimony in our legal system. . . . Our sense of the normative is nourished in narrative, but so is our sense of breach and of exception" (Bruner 1990, 97). This mediation between "normative" and "exception" is much like the mediation between life and death that Egan (1988) describes. We also could consider this the mediation between the known and the unknown.

It becomes increasingly clear how important a holistic mindset is to learning if we are to negotiate between the known and the unknown. Imagination and story combine to give us the skills to manage both known and unknown and build a continuum that helps us get from one to the other. The use of story in learning is certainly not new to higher education. The technologies that can help us tell stories are evolving, however, and it is important to use these new technologies to bring forward the relevance and meaning of stories.

Another type of storytelling that new technologies are making possible is gaming. The New Media Consortium's (Massively Multiplayer, 2007) *2007 Horizon Report* cites educational use of gaming as one to watch on the three- to five-year horizon, and research is already being done in this area. One important piece of gaming that aids learning is the fact that most games are stories. They contain characters (usually the players themselves as avatars), settings, rules, plot, and drama. Gaming is not a topic of this particular book, but it is important to at least note the connection that exists between storytelling and gaming and to suggest that while future study of gaming in learning will address many issues, it will likely address the idea of story, too.

DIGITAL STORIES IN THE CLASSROOM

While Egan (1988) and others have provided some of the theoretical frameworks for understanding the use of story in formal education and in navigating our lives, let's consider the more specific uses of digital storytelling in particular. The University of Houston's College of Education has outlined specific goals and objectives of digital storytelling in an academic environment. They note that digital storytelling "can appeal to diverse learning styles . . . generate interest . . . capitalize on the creative talents of . . . students . . . [and] publish student work" (University of Houston, College of Education n.d., para. 2). Digital stories can be implemented in classrooms as hooks to set up lessons or to stimulate discussion or as writing prompts. Creating digital stories also can be assigned to students, for instance to research an idea from a particular point of view

This dual use of digital stories in an academic environment highlights some of the reasons that community can be so helpful. Assigning the creation of digital stories is a complex matter, and a single instructor might not be equipped to guide students in every facet of story making. Technical, graphic, or compositional support may need to be brought in to assist class efforts. Alternately, if stories that already exist are going to be shown in classes as an educational hook or to supplement a lesson, instructors will need to know what already exists. There are specific Web sites (see Appendix) that provide links to stories, and there are megasites, such as *YouTube*, where digital stories are little gold nuggets hidden amid vast warehouses of video but may not always be easily identified as digital stories. This makes finding appropriate stories for the classroom challenging. A community built around digital storytelling will help instructors know what is being produced in other classes that might be of interest in their own class, and it will help them discover where such stories are being stored. This furthers the sense of community by hearing what other students at the same university have told.

As instructional hooks, digital stories can revolve around the topic of the class for the day or even the semester. One colleague created a very short video that she used to set the tone for a freshman seminar about researching controversial issues online. Through this piece, she was able to set the tone for a course focused on searching for information rather than on exacting truth. Another colleague learned the technique of digital storytelling by examining her cultural development growing up in Sierra Leone where her gold earrings had to be refitted each year so that they would grow with her. The story was a beautiful description of growing up in another culture, and she used the metaphor of the earring to differentiate her own growing up from her American-born daughter's growing up in the United States. This story could easily be useful in starting discussion in a cultural studies or women's studies class.

Critique can be another educational use of a digital story. A staff member who participated in one of our story circles created a workshop activity centered on a digital story she had produced (Heather Mitchell April 12, 2007, personal communication). In her workshop, each student in a small group of four is assigned a different part of the story to focus on: the words, the images, the music, or the storyteller. Each student reflects on and writes a one-minute paper on how that element tells the story. Here are examples of reactions students might have: the music can convey energy, emotion, confusion, simple rhythms that become more complex; the images might be bold, colorful, prolific, minimalist, or they might linger, or they might be fast-paced; the words can be poetic, gentle, harsh, or introduce new vocabulary; the storyteller's voice is personally invested or distant. The four students then share their reflections within their small group and follow up by developing short lists of similarities and differences for the story components. Finally, the small group discussions merge into a facilitated large group discussion in which the small groups report out their lists.

Alternatively, this could be an individual assignment in which each student considers all the components and writes a reflective comparison paper on them, as well as how the story seemed the same or different when experiencing it as a whole and as parts. For an assignment completed outside of class time, the requirements and time allotted of course would be greater. It also is possible to imagine a combined use of the two ideas Mitchell proposes. The group assignment could be used in class to orient students to the process, and the individual assignment could be used to assess the student's understanding of the digital storytelling process, critical thinking, and analytical skills.

Students can also be assigned to create their own digital stories. Students might be asked to write about themselves or about an academic topic, preferably placing themselves within the story. They might use the project to engage in civic activity to document stories of people in their community, as students at the University of Maryland, Baltimore Campus, New Media Center (2007) did when they helped retirement home residents tell their own stories. Students provided the technical and artistic work, while residents supplied old photos and artifacts and narrated their stories.

On our own campus some students in an introductory biology class made a digital story as an alternative to a written assignment on an academic topic. Working with a graduate assistant trained in the technology and using the facilities of the high tech media center on campus, two groups of students created two separate stories. One had to do with the biological effect that music has on our brains, the other with how insects breathe. This assignment was one option offered to a large-enrollment class of non-majors to engage students in a biology topic through an appealing learning method. The students had to do quite a bit of research to develop a script and visual representations of scientific ideas to create these short videos.

The story, *How Do Insects Breathe?*, purposely used lots of humor, with one of the students dressing up as "Frank the Ferocious Fly" and serving as an erratic narrator, much as one would expect from a fly. Because this was a group project, students divided up the jobs of contributing art representations, writing the script, running the camera, editing, and adding voices to various parts of the narrative. The overall style was a bit camp and mimicked somewhat the didactic nature of old filmstrips.

While the title of the video asked a question, it was not a dramatic question. In fact, a dramatic question in this context might not be answerable. Here are some that the students could have grappled with: What does insect breath feel like? Can an insect enjoy the feeling of a deep breath that sucks in the smell of baking cinnamon rolls or of a gasp of air after finally surfacing from a deep dive to the bottom of a pool? These are questions that inspire wondering, that might not have scientific answer, but that could make illuminating the anatomy of a lungless insect a bit more thought-provoking. These questions put the storyteller inside the story. They allow the listener to engage in some of that mediation between the known and the unknown that we have been talking about.

While humor often is a perfectly acceptable and even a welcome attribute of a story, engagement based on camp will not lead to deep thinking. We were not present in that group process, so we cannot attest to how the story circle went, if in fact there was one. Based on the script, however, it seems likely that the script-writing process focused mainly on getting the facts straight. Often to find that dramatic question, a group needs to talk not only to each other, but also to their audience to learn what might engage the audience and what aspects of the story pique the audience's curiosity most. To achieve deep learning the story circle should be an important component of the digital storytelling process, or a movie based solely on fact and less on deep thinking will develop. The criteria the instructor lays out will greatly impact this type of outcome.

If students are assigned to create a digital story for a class, it is important to provide them with clear criteria. Here are some questions that can help guide an instructor's thinking on what type of criteria might be used:

- How important is the story? (Engagement and composition)
- How important are the facts?
- How important is the use of technology?
- How important are creative details?
- How long should it be?
- Do you want to provide the dramatic question or have the students find it themselves?
- Will they work in groups or alone?

In a composition course, general composition issues will certainly be important. In a biology course, the accuracy of the science or the accuracy of metaphors used to illustrate a scientific fact may be of primary importance. In a film class, how the video is filmed and edited, and the technical issues of sound quality and photograph quality might be most important.

When it is time to assess the digital stories, it is important to match the assessment with these criteria. It is also useful to keep in mind the technology skills that students start the process with and what sort of supplementary technical expertise they have available. A fun assessment component could include hosting a class showcase and allowing students to vote for their favorite video. Many students enjoy posting videos to *YouTube* just for the enjoyment of seeing how popular it becomes and what sort of feedback it receives. This would be one way of measuring popularity and getting a certain kind of feedback locally.

Mitchell's (April 12, 2007, personal communication) exercises outlined earlier also could serve as a grading rubric for instructors. Stories could be evaluated on the four components of music, images, script, and storyteller. Then a summative evaluation of how these work together could be offered. An alternate rubric might be one based upon the seven elements. Depending on the course in which a digital story is assigned, another element in a grading rubric might include how well the story reflects the subject matter it was meant to enlighten. For instance, in a history class a digital story might be created to provide personal perspective on an historical event. While storytellers might take on fictitious personae to place themselves in history, the perspective must ring true to what is known about the event. A digital story done for a biology class, such as the one aforementioned, should accurately reflect the known scientific data.

Criteria for assessing digital stories in an academic environment have not yet been codified or even developed into a set of best practices because the technology for classroom use is so new. One example of an assessment or evaluation rubric for digital stories, however, is given on the University of Houston's (n.d.) digital storytelling Web site on educational uses for digital storytelling. Houston's rubric evaluates students on the following items:

- Purpose of Story
- Point of View
- Dramatic Question
- Choice of Content

- Clarity of Voice
- Pacing of Narrative
- Meaningful Audio Soundtrack
- Quality of Images
- Economy of Story Detail
- Grammar and Language Usage

Likely, others will develop over time.

FACULTY STORIES

Beyond stories by students, another powerful kind of story is the kind created by faculty themselves. Digital stories can be a new way for faculty to introduce themselves to students at the beginning of a course or to provide some personal insights during the quarter or semester. Faculty can show these stories to students as models when assigning a storytelling project to them, or, they can show them along with student stories in a showcase of class stories.

Digital stories allow instructors to show their humanity to students and to their colleagues. This can be a difficult thing to do, especially if faculty see their role as being that of an expert leader. On the other hand, sharing stories can be an enriching mentoring process to help students understand the experiences and passions that have led faculty to become expert in their fields. Most successful faculty probably already bring some personal aspects to their teaching. Dramatizing that humanity can lead students to trust, engage with, and approach faculty more readily.

If creating their own digital stories alongside their students, faculty can use the safety net of the story circle to explore the personal in a way that engages their listeners but is appropriate to their relationship with their students while still allowing them to stretch their own comfort zones. A practical benefit is that faculty participation shows students that faculty know how to use the technology and thus are in a position to authoritatively assess student work.

PROFESSIONAL LIFE

Ultimately, of course, higher education is meant to prepare students for lifelong learning in their future professional and personal lives. Students will need to take these theories, lessons, and technologies and learn to apply them in new ways in the working world. Just as higher education is being impacted by social and other technologies so are many professions. Schoolteachers are bringing these technologies to younger grades. Physicians are seeing technology and business practices transform the way they work. Journalists are learning to rely on social technologies to gather and report news. The person who can use the technologies to help steer their professions in this new environment in meaningful ways will be prized. Students need to carry not only facts, data, and scientific knowledge into the working world but also metaphorical and cultural knowledge in order to mediate the changing worlds of their professions.

In a presentation he gave to University of Maryland, Baltimore Campus workshop participants, Lambert (2006) discusses the emergence of a new sort of interdisciplinary skill that can begin in college with digital storytelling, bringing new skills to the workforce. He describes how skills in social work, communications, media and composition can combine to create a "digital storytelling facilitator." Such a person can help give voice to those in society who might not be able to manage this process on their own, such as the elderly or the disabled.

While many professions are being affected, Brown, Denning, Groh, and Prusak (2001) discuss at length how important story is in the organizations that employ professionals. Stories aid in illuminating what lies beneath the surface of the organization. Denning, for instance, notes that "What we discovered was of course was that there is huge divide between the things that are visible and discernible in the organization i.e. the facts, the actions, the policies, and the things are that are invisible and intangible, i.e. the values, the attitudes, the narratives, the life narratives. We spend most of our time in organizations talking and thinking about the visible and discernible things, even though it is the invisible values and attitudes and narratives that are actually driving most of what is going on" (Denning 2001, *Storytelling not Story* section, para. 3). Through finding what this narrative is and turning it into the act of storytelling it is possible to unearth some of these hidden attributes. The communal process of storytelling allows values and attitudes to be examined, discussed, and even imparted, across organizations.

On the same Web site, Prusak (2001) examines the elements he considers to be useful in organizational storytelling. His elements are "endurance, salience, sense-making and comfort-level." While these do not match specifically Lambert's (2002) seven elements of digital storytelling, they do match well the learning theories suggested by McDrury and Alterio (2003) and provide guidance to the would-be storyteller. In the realm of organizational storytelling there is often an agenda to steer thinking. The agenda has to start with exposing realities in a nonthreatening and nonaccusatory way, something stories can do. The end purpose of organizational storytelling may differ from a more general approach to digital storytelling, but all stories must contain one specific component to be effective and interesting, that is, "[c]reative abrasion . . . [by which] ideas . . . really rub against each other productively as opposed to destructively" (Brown 2001, *The Knowledge Ecology of Xerox PARC* section, para. 4). This is much the same role that Lambert's "dramatic question" (Lambert 2002, xi) plays.

In this day of rapidly changing technology and increased globalization academia, industry, and individuals all are faced on many fronts with the need to mediate between the known and the unknown. "Storytelling is especially important in periods of cultural and technological transition, since it has a robustness and flexibility that other means of organizing experience generally lack" (Sax 2006, 149). This social transition has many academics experimenting with and applying technology in the classroom.

What does it mean to education that students are wired, that they network online, that they increasingly spend more hours on a computer than watching television? How does this affect what and how we teach? Digital storytelling provides a bridge between tradition and technology. "The great teachers of pre-industrial times such as Aesop, Socrates, and Jesus were all primarily storytellers, not providers of information," writes Sax (2006, 105). Drawing from this ancient tradition, digital storytelling can encourage academia to embrace the new.

Stories are universal. Stories are educational. Stories help us reflect and learn deeply. One colleague who participated in an early workshop asked us if we thought the emotional component of digital storytelling ran counter to most academic discourse. Indeed we do. And indeed, that is precisely the role of stories in academia. They can return us to our humanity, to the why of our work, to the passion behind our intellect.

REFERENCES

Barr, R. B. and Tagg, J. (1995). From teaching to learning—a new paradigm for undergraduate education. *Change*, November/December, 13–25. Retrieved April 9, 2007, from http://critical.tamucc.edu/~blalock/readings/tch2learn.htm.

Barrett, H. C. (2004). *Electronic portfolios as digital stories of deep learning: Emerging digital tool to support reflection in learner-centered portfolios.*

Retrieved June 13, 2007, from http://electronicportfolios.com/digistory/epstory.html.

Brown, J. S. Denning, S., Groh, K., and Prusak, L. (2001). *Storytelling: Passport to success in the 21st century*. Retrieved June 13, 2007, from http://www.creatingthe21stcentury.org/index.html.

———. (2001). Storytelling: Scientist's perspective. Retrieved June 13, 2007, from Brown, J. S., Denning, S., Groh, K., and Prusak, L. *Storytelling: Passport to success in the 21st century*, http://www.creatingthe21stcentury.org/JSB11-Ecology-PARC.html.

Bruner, J. S. (1990). *Acts of meaning*. Cambridge, MA: Harvard University Press.

DeBell, M. and Chapman, C. (2006). *Computer and Internet use by students in 2003* (NCES 2006–065). U.S. Department of Education. Washington, DC: National Center for Education Statistics.

Denning, S. (2001). Storytelling to ignite change. Retrieved June 13, 2007, from Brown, J. S., Denning, S., Groh, K., and Prusak, L. *Storytelling: Passport to success in the 21st century*, http://www.creatingthe21stcentury.org/Steve13-storytelling-not-story.html.

Duch, B. (1996). *Problems: A key factor in PBL*. Retrieved June 13, 2007, from http://www.udel.edu/pbl/cte/spr96-phys.html.

Egan, K. (1988). *Teaching as story telling: An alternative approach to teaching and the curriculum*. London: Routledge.

Herreid, C. F. (1998). *What makes a good case: Some basic rules of good storytelling help teachers generate student excitement in the classroom*. Retrieved June 13, 2007, from http://ublib.buffalo.edu/libraries/projects/cases/teaching/good-case.html. (Originally appeared in the *Journal of College Science Teaching*, 27, 163–165.)

Kellner, D. (1998). Multiple literacies and critical pedagogy in a multicultural society. *Educational Theory*, 48, 103–122. Retrieved June 13, 2007, from Academic Search Complete. http://proxy.lib.ohio-state.edu/login?url=http://search.ebscohost.com/login.aspx?direct=true&db=a9h&AN=430092&site=ehost-live.

Lambert, J. (2002). *Digital storytelling: Capturing lives, creating community*. Berkeley, CA: Digital Diner Press.

———. (January 13, 2006). *Incorporating digital storytelling into teaching and learning* (Presentation, University of Maryland, Baltimore County, January 13, 2006). Retrieved June 13, 2007, from http://asp1.umbc.edu/newmedia/studio/stream/qtdetail.cfm?recordID=388.

McDrury, J. and Alterio, M. (2003). *Learning through storytelling in higher education*. Sterling, VA: Kogan Page.

New Media Consortium. (January 23, 2007). Critical challenges. *2007 Horizon Report*. Retrieved June 13, 2007, from http://www.nmc.org/horizon/2007/critical-challenges.

————. (January 23, 2007). Four to five years: Massively multiplayer educational gaming. *2007 Horizon Report*. Retrieved June 13, 2007, from http://www.nmc.org/horizonproject/2007/massively-multiplayer-educational-gaming.

————. (January 23, 2007). Technologies to watch. *2007 Horizon Report*. Retrieved June 13, 2007, from http://www.nmc.org/horizon/2007/technologies-watch.

Pink, D. H. (2005). *A whole new mind: moving from the information age to the conceptual age*. New York: Riverhead Books.

Prusak, L. (2001) *The attributes of story*. Retrieved June 13, 2007, from Brown, J., Denning, S., Groh, K., and Prusak, L. S*torytelling: Passport to the 21st century*, http://www.creatingthe21stcentury.org/Larry-IV-attributes.html.

Rhem, J. (1998). Problem-based learning: an introduction. *National Teaching and Learning Forum*, 8. Retrieved April 15, 2007, from http://www.ntlf.com/html/pi/9812/pbl_1.htm.

Sax, B. (2006). Storytelling in a liminal time [electronic version]. *On the Horizon*, 14, 147–151.

Street, B. (2003). What's "new" in new literacy studies? Critical approaches to literacy in theory and practice [electronic version]. *Current Issues in Comparative Education*, 5, 77–91.

University of Houston, College of Education (n.d.). *Educational uses of digital storytelling*. Retrieved June 13, 2007, from http://www.coe.uh.edu/digital-storytelling/.

University of Maryland, Baltimore Campus, New Media Center. (n.d.). *Digital stories at UMBC*. Retrieved June 13, 2007, from http://umbc.edu/oit/newmedia/studio/digitalstories/.

Wesch, M. (January 31, 2007). *Web 2.0 . . . How the Web is us/ing us*. Retrieved June 13, 2007, from http://www.youtube.com/watch?v=6gmP4nk0EOE.

Young, J. R. (2007). An anthropologist explores the culture of video blogging [electronic version]. *Chronicle of Higher Education*, 53, A42.

CHAPTER 5
Social Technologies, Stories, and Libraries

If digital storytelling has a role in the classroom, what sort of role might it play in the academic library? Given the era of "Googlization", a crisis in scholarly communication, information overload, a cross-disciplinary interest in information literacy, and increasing virtual access to collections and services and the resulting alleged decrease in the need for library as place, stories may play a more important role than might be perceived on a surface level. The library is unique among campus units. It is both a support unit and a teaching and learning unit, so digital storytelling might be used by libraries not only for teaching and learning purposes, but also for internal organizational development, for marketing and external development, as well as outreach to the campus community and beyond.

In libraries, social technologies stretch the meaning of information, challenge notions of authority and bias, and heighten issues of copyright compliance. User-created content mixes with traditional sources of information to challenge notions of information literacy. Additionally, libraries have adopted the notion of Web 2.0 into their own terminology, resulting in the term *Library 2.0* to describe how these new user-centered technologies revolutionize the way we function.

Library 2.0 has been defined in various ways, but one definition is particularly pertinent to a discussion of digital storytelling in libraries. Maness (2006) lists four essential elements of *Library 2.0*:

- It is user-centered.
- It provides a multimedia experience.
- It is socially rich.
- It is communally innovative (para. 7).

His inclusion of multimedia is somewhat different from other definitions, but is particularly apt for our purposes. Certainly, all these characteristics apply to digital storytelling, thus making digital storytelling
a type of *Library 2.0* technology.

STUDENT RESEARCH

Understanding some of the realities of student research habits is a helpful beginning for exploring the role of digital stories in the library.
Students today are certainly not underwhelmed with access to information. The days of the librarian as gatekeeper are gone. Information
flows so quickly and easily that instead students (indeed all of us) are
faced with information riches and overload. The most common tool
that students use for navigating this wealth are search engines, the most
notable being *Google*. This leaves faculty and librarians frustrated with
student research outcomes, even as our own daily use of *Google* belies
the handiness and value of this tool.

One hallmark of the era of *Google* research is the decontextualized
search for information. Information on every topic and of every type is
spidered into a massive net. Searching is done by key word. Although
ranked for relevancy, disparate sites result. Quick answers abound, but
deeply contextualized knowledge is hard to come by. In fact, by settling
for quick answers researchers may be passing up the chance to think
deeply about what they find.

Just as *Google* dominated the research efforts of students for the first
five years of the decade, *Wikipedia* now seems poised to be the new
Google for students. *Wikipedia* is in some respects a helpful addition to
the information landscape because at least it recontextualizes information. In fact, many searches in *Google* now produce a *Wikipedia* entry
close to the top of the results list. Look up the word *work* in *Wikipedia*
and you will start with a "disambiguation" (*Wikipedia* 2007) page,
where words that have multiple meanings help separate the various
meanings and lead the user into what is relevant.

Many librarians, however, denounce *Wikipedia's* lack of authority.
We hear of professors deriding the use of *Wikipedia* for research papers,
and in some cases banning *Wikipedia* citations from papers altogether;

although one study (Giles 2005) has shown that *Wikipedia* is generally as accurate as *The Encyclopedia Britannica* for science topics. Another indicates (Wilkinson and Huberman 2007) that the more an article has been edited by a variety of people, the more accurate it becomes.

The difficulty with *Wikipedia* that most professors dislike, however, is that the information is shallow, like what one would find in a general encyclopedia. The entries may be broad in scope, provide good context, but may lack depth and may not answer the specific question at hand. They can be a bit like the old joke of asking your father what time it is and instead being told how the clock works. While students' appreciation for a topic may be expanded and enlightened, their original questions may remain unanswered. And if answered, the answers certainly are not the student's own answers, constructed by synthesizing new information into the student's own knowledge base. This has always been a problem when using encyclopedias for college level research. Encyclopedias have long been taught in library instruction as good background material with which students can ground themselves on a topic before beginning actual research. As that sort of tool *Wikipedia* can be helpful. With "featured article" (Wikipedia 2007) status granted to those articles that are balanced, well written, and well documented, and with the studies showing that the reliability of *Wikipedia* entries ranks well compared to other supposedly more authoritative sources, there is some level of agreement that *Wikipedia* at least is a good starting point.

Perhaps what frustrates many academics about students accessing *Wikipedia* and *Google* for research is that absolutely no prethinking is required. Plunk in a keyword, pull out an answer, just like with a vending machine. With most other traditional library resources, some thinking has to happen ahead of time. What discipline is likely to publish on the topic? What type of source likely would contain the needed information: a newspaper article, a government study, or a scholarly treatise? Are quick facts needed, or a whole book? Is this an exhaustive search or a representative one? What other terms might a person use to say the same thing? In what other contexts might this topic be addressed? When students do reach a frustration level with Googling and wikiing for answers and finally approach a librarian for help, such are the kinds of questions the librarian will ask before proceeding to search.

Only research that requires critical thinking will help students learn. Mega-searches that pull in everything, ensuring only that something will be found whether relevant or not; and cutting and pasting text, rather than taking time to process the information do not lead to reflection and do not offer the opportunity for meaning-making. Such is the crisis of modern student research.

How then can critical thinking remain a component of student research as the search tools become easier and easier to use but less discriminating? The primary answer is that research assignments themselves need to be well structured to be meaningful. While the course instructor bears ultimate responsibility for this, librarians can provide a helpful perspective. Librarians can provide suggestions for structuring the research component in meaningful ways because of their insights on what is and what is not effective and efficient research. There are a variety of other instructional support roles librarians can play as well.

Where does digital storytelling fit into this? Librarians often talk to classes about doing research. Often these sessions are packed with information about searching and databases and citing sources. Sometimes the presentations are laced with humor, games, and candy. But how often do librarians use their limited time to slow down and ask students to take a minute to think? What if librarians presented stories about how the *Oxford English Dictionary* came to be, or how six tractor trailers were needed to get a special collection from someone's home to the library, or how and why a librarian came to write a *Wikipedia* entry, or how reading a book on a topic not only changed a librarian's understanding of the topic, but changed him as well? If librarians told stories, digital or otherwise, could they begin to reinsert a moment of thought into students understanding of research and open them to expectation and discovery beyond the vending machine model?

In 2000 the video *e-literate* (University of California–Los Angeles) became the talk of librarians teaching information literacy everywhere. This groundbreaking use of video to teach library skills excited librarians who quickly realized the potential of this medium. An extensive report on the impact of the video prepared by the University of California–Los Angeles, Graduate School of Education and Information Science (2003) showed that 290 respondents saw the value of using a short video as part of a larger presentation to students as an engaging introduction and as an aid in eliciting critical thinking.

The beauty of a digital story is that it can be saved and reused in a variety of classrooms for a variety of purposes. The librarian who knows or cares about something in particular might not be the person giving the lecture that day, might be retired, or have moved on to work for a different institution. A digital story can be shown to a class where no librarian has ever been invited before. It may be an online course that involves no face-to-face lectures at all. A digital story can lend a human touch otherwise lacking in library instruction. A digital story can help the students pause and consider that an information resource had to be created, by people, and for a reason.

Another crisis of modern research, at least as librarians see it, is the demise of the reference desk. First came a precipitous drop in the number of reference transactions encountered at reference desks. Now there are questions as to whether the reference desk will remain in academic libraries, with one librarian predicting their demise by 2012 (Carlson 2007, para. 9) as librarians increasingly meet the more limited number of student research needs through online chat, e-mail, and text messaging. As library systems developers strive to provide seamless access to resources, librarians are left with even fewer opportunities to interact with students. In this technology driven environment, it is quite possible for students, faculty, and even university administration to forget that there are people behind information resources at all, people who care about information, about education, and about students. Digital stories can be one reminder of the human beings behind the library's Web presence.

INFORMATION LITERACY

The Association of College and Research Libraries (2007, para. 5) defines *information literacy* as a set of abilities requiring individuals to "recognize when information is needed and have the ability to locate, evaluate, and use effectively the needed information." While concise, this definition represents a wide range of skills. It is possible to look at these skills and think that they can easily be boiled down to a checklist of dos and don'ts that makes a student information literate. Such a list is necessary for assessment purposes and to help map out teaching methods, but it does not address the more intangible aspects of information literacy. Ward indicates that information literacy "also demands that we know how to manage information in more creative and meaningful ways. Growth in reflection and self-knowledge, for instance, is just as important as critical thinking to the development of information literacy. The two sides complement each other and are inextricably linked" (Ward 2006, 396).

On her wiki, *Information Fluency Meets Web 2.0*, teacher-librarian Joyce Kasman Valenza (2007) includes both digital storytelling and "beyond PowerPoint" presentation skills as important tools in the practice and teaching of information fluency, a term often used synonymously with information literacy. Among the wealth of links provided to audio and video of prominent journalists, speakers, and authors discussing the art of conveying a message are many that remind us of Lambert's (2002) seven elements of digital storytelling. One blog posting states, "presentations are about the transfer of emotion not just facts. Facts are a necessary condition, but they are rarely sufficient. If it were only about facts, we could just send an email and cancel most presentations" (blog posting http://presentationzen.blogs.com/, May 22, 2007). In general, Valenza's wiki and its links lead librarians to realize that we must incorporate a variety of techniques to improve the presentations we give regarding information literacy.

It is not surprising that increasingly not everyone thinks information literacy belongs just to libraries. If we move outside of a library-centric point of view, the understanding of what it means to be information literate widens. As one information literate student points out, "For the average college student . . . [the listing of specific skills] sounds like a page from a course syllabus or a talking point on a tour of the university's library. The idea of evaluating information and then using it to accomplish a specific task may seem to hold little relevance beyond merely looking for sources for a class research paper or evaluating the merit of an unattributed Web site. But the core principles of information literacy—access, evaluation, use—crisscross with nearly every technology that the average college student will use on a daily basis, even those used for managing their personal lives" (Windham 2006, 4). Shapiro and Hughes (1996, para. 5) also argue for a broader understanding of information literacy, asking, "[S]hould it be something broader, something that enables individuals not only to use information and information technology effectively and adapt to their constant changes but also to think critically about the entire information enterprise and information society? Something more akin to a 'liberal art'—knowledge that is part of what it means to be a free person in the present historical context of the dawn of the information age?"

In other words, not only definitions, but also academic understanding of the meaning of information literacy must evolve beyond those very specific library research skills needed to accomplish course assignments. The lines of scholarly research and personal research are blurring for students. Issues of privacy as they place information on *Facebook* or *MySpace*; issues of copyright as they download images, movies, and music; issues of reliability of information are all things that students need to know about for personal reasons and that are not merely academic topics. In the era of massive self-publication through blogs, wikis, *Flickr*, and *YouTube*, discernment of how information travels where it does becomes important in questioning issues of accuracy, bias, and authority. Helping students understand these issues in the personal realm might be a good starting point for taking these issues into the academic realm. Challenging students to understand economic models of information might help them understand why there are appropriate and inappropriate ways to use information they find online. Contextualizing reasons, creating metaphors and scenarios—that is, telling stories—can be an engaging and meaningful way to help students navigate information literacy.

If we expand our understanding of what information literacy is to the more varied set of literacies that Shapiro and Hughes (1996) propose, then not only are stories a valuable way to teach reflectively, but library stories from students, faculty, staff, librarians, and the greater community can become part of a broader tapestry of material for reflective and rich consideration of information. And while a variety of approaches are needed for encouraging information literacy, digital storytelling can be one approach.

INFORMATION OVERLOAD

Sax (2006) argues that stories have always been a means for people to cope with information overload. Before the written word, stories were used as a device to organize information in a way that could be passed down and remembered. Advances in knowledge indexing and finding aids marked the industrial age. But now knowledge creation has advanced to such a rate that our finding aids, while becoming more powerful and accurate, are providing less context and meaning.

Beyond the increased flow of information, the 2003 *OCLC Membership Report* on "Five-Year Information Format Trends" indicates that libraries are managing an increasing variety of formats such as pdf files, Web pages, and mp3 files, just as users are adopting new information technologies such as smart phones, cell phones, and mp3 players. This report has led to more frequent use of the phrase "content not container" which recognizes that we are looking at increasingly "chunked" information whose provenance may be difficult to determine. Stories linked to content or to finding aids can complement these formats, tools, and content. A story about a collector, the subject, or the history of a collection could be linked to a finding aid for the collection.

How many analysts have determined that the flow of information to the average person has removed the "gate" from the idea of "librarian as gatekeeper"? Librarians do not need to facilitate access to information any more. This leaves students more vulnerable to information overload. At the same time, as Pink (2005) suggests, students need a more whole-brained and cohesive approach to information gathering. This means that libraries now must be concerned with developing in students Pink's (2005) more right-brained aptitudes of "artistry, empathy, sense-making, and emotional connection." Managing information can no longer be our only occupation. We must incorporate new roles of helping users find meaning in information, care about it, and develop empathy from it.

SCHOLARLY COMMUNICATION

It is worth mentioning the potential role of digital stories in the scholarly communication process. Recall the story referred to in Chapter 2 in which a faculty member from our institution attended a digital storytelling workshop and created a story about his research into imaginative inquiry in the elementary classroom. His story took place in a particular classroom where he had been invited to work with the children to implement his theory. In his story he told about the project the children worked on, the questions they grappled with, and how all this fit into his theory of more meaningful learning for students. Now when he presents at conferences, he shows this story as part of his presentation and engages his audiences in ways he has not been able to before. Now his audiences ask different types of questions.

Another workshop participant has been involved with a digital archiving project for a student gender identity group on campus. She is working with the libraries to store this archive in our institutional repository. She created a digital story in our workshop about her connection to this group, what meaning this archiving project has for her personally and for the student group, and how documenting this particular community could benefit it. Her own story will be stored with the archive and will be able to serve as a personal, not institutional or academic, introduction to the project, giving voice, meaning, and purpose to the collection.

These are only two examples of the use of digital stories in the realm of scholarly communication that are worth further exploration. The notion of engaging peers and researchers in new ways is one provocative use of digital stories. If peers know about the personal connection the creators have to their work, will it lead them to ask questions about the work that they might not ask otherwise? If researchers in disparate fields can engage and connect in this personal way, will it lead to collaborations and common understandings across disciplines that might not have been discovered otherwise? Can the library facilitate this cross-fertilization through digital storytelling workshops and new discovery tools? These questions are worth future investigation.

COLLECTIONS

Increasingly, library shelves may not represent all that the library owns. More and more of what libraries own is either being relegated to a remote storage facility (quite common in research libraries) or is available online. Not only are an increasing number of databases and journals available electronically, but so are reference works, digitized special collections, and books. Library users easily can lose track of the fact that these are library collections because the collections do not reside in our buildings and because users can access them from their homes.

Libraries have long identified themselves by the collections they hold. As collections disperse and apparently vaporize, libraries begin to lose their identities. Subject specialists who oversee particular collections struggle with how to manage physical collections. Should the disciplines be separated out into easy to browse subsections? Doing so helps brand the collection and can build a community of researchers who all might gather in the physical space for research. But sometimes this separation confuses more casual or cross-disciplinary users. Sometimes there is a lack of space to build such units.

Digital stories about collections can help organize collections virtually and can help build communities of researchers. An intersection of librarian, faculty, and student stories about facets of a collection that can be found in appropriate online venues can help researchers get to know each other's research interests and what they have discovered through the collections. The ability to link out in multiple directions allows a story to be part of more than just one collection. The digital story that introduces the gender identity digital archiving project described above also shows how stories can help to frame a collection. Such stories can introduce the purpose, history, and context of a collection. Stories can restore the sense of place lost when a collection is no longer in print or centralized in one physical space.

LIBRARY AS PLACE

Libraries are reinventing many of their spaces. Learning commons, coffee bars, collaborative worktables, wireless computing areas, exhibit areas, and quiet study areas are some of the special places into which we are welcoming users. In the more social areas, plasma screens might be incorporated as a place to show library stories and illuminate our collections, services, and the many opportunities for discovery and learning that otherwise might not be apparent to casual library users. This use of plasma screens would mimic other social environments where people have become accustomed to watching news or music videos, but libraries can provide content that is more directly meaningful when viewed in the library setting. A digital story by an exhibit's curator can engage casual visitors and draw them into the exhibit. Digital stories can provide a bridge between the known casual uses of the library and the deeper, richer, and more mysterious aspects of collections and expertise that are not so apparent.

Just as the academic library has traditionally bridged the university's social and academic physical spaces, so can digital stories bridge these mental spaces for students. Stories stemming from the academic, but incorporating the personal, are ideal for display in the social spaces of the academic library.

Searing and Lucht review many articles that discuss the physical changes, needs, and creature comforts of the library as place. This overview makes clear that a multiplicity of functions and accommodations are needed in libraries today. While libraries are still places for quiet reading and reflection, that is not all that they are. In fact, "[d]igital image and sound are becoming as important as text. The distinction between libraries, audiovisual centers and production studios is blurring" (Searing and Lucht 2006, 5).

LIBRARIES AND COMMUNITY

Digital stories can help us expose and tap into the deeper human needs that libraries traditionally have helped society address. Chief among these needs is the need for community. Consider how public libraries have supported the needs of and contributed to the meaning of community. They have educated immigrants, fed the imagination of youth, and helped the public to be more enlightened consumers. Through "One Book" common reading initiatives, branch libraries in public schools, and similar programs, public libraries now are extending their reach beyond just the users who come through their doors to develop the whole community's sense of itself. A recent *New York Times* article (Winerip 2007) describes how many parents turn to the public library when they are trying to help their children work through problems such as fear, divorce, health, and death. Real life stories help both children and adults cope with their problems by seeing how others coped and found resolution. The stories in the library's books provide readers with a communal experience and provide them with other perspectives.

Academic libraries are spaces for informal, nonclassroom learning. People learn by reading or talking over a cup of coffee, so coffee bars have entered library buildings. Students find information better when comparing strategies and brainstorming together, so the walls of study carrels have come down, and tables with space for more than one person around a computer workstation have replaced them. Learning is social; community is essential to learning. Libraries are not quiet anymore.

Community is both externally and internally directed. Externally, libraries consider relationships with their users. What do users know that others might wish to learn? What happens to users when they interact with a library's collections? What do learners care about? Who do they become? Increasingly, library users do not necessarily enter library buildings physically, but instead just use library services from a distance. Who are these people? Do they know who we in the libraries are? Is a library just a bunch of bits and bytes, or do people still work there? If so, who are these people? What exactly do they do? Why do people work in libraries? Answers to these questions help users know what to expect from the library and help the library know what users need. This sort of understanding is essential to directing library evolution and growth. Stories are one way to begin answering some of these questions.

Libraries need community for ongoing support, as well. All libraries need to develop relationships not only with constituents who use that system's services but also with those who can contribute to its goals. In our increasingly Googlized society, we can no longer take the role of the library for granted. Taxpayers want to know why it is worth increasing the funding for their local library. Campus administrators want a rationale for investing in both library buildings and wireless access. Successful donor appeals rarely happen without careful culti-vation and provision of evidence of need and good stewardship on the part of the library.

Digital stories can contribute to all these relationships. They can bring public library "One Book" programs to life and enhance the social environment of academic libraries. Digital stories can help us answer questions about the library and its staff for our users, and—when created by our users—can answer our questions about them, too. Digital stories can help a donor get to know a curator and hear how learners are interacting with our collections in our spaces. Stories now can allow prospective students into the world of a special collection to learn about the lives behind the artifacts, the photos, the letters and manuscripts.

Internally, libraries are also organizations in need of community. One academic librarian bemoans the specialization and splintering that has occurred in our large institutions and has made us strangers to our colleagues (Smith 2003). We fester and fight for our own pieces of the pie, resenting what our colleagues get instead of us, rather than seeing our institutions as whole and each person's expertise, talent, and effort as valuable parts of the entire and complex organization. Stories can unify by clarifying our diversity. Stories can remind us of what other people are doing that is different than what we are doing and how much richer the organization is for their efforts.

Brown (2005) appreciates the importance of the use of story for problem solving and development within organizations. When organizations face developmental problems, he notes, "[t]hese two elements—the context and the moral [or point]—enable you to apply the story to a new situation, and sometimes many new situations." (65) Stories in organizations can provide direction for a way to develop or insights into how to solve problems. Building community internally as well as externally is important to the health, growth, and the direction of our organizations.

VIDEO AND LIBRARIES

Is it appropriate for libraries to be in the business of creating videos, telling stories, helping others tell theirs, and promoting visual literacy? Are libraries only about books and collecting content others have made? Consider film collections, art libraries, cartoon collections, theater set collections. Consider exhibits, brochures, and guides. Libraries have collected multiple formats over the years and have articulated what is in their collections in multiple ways. Digital stories are a new way to articulate what we have, only now it is not just about articulating our collections, services, and expertise, but also about articulating what they mean and why they matter, both to us and to our users.

Historically, much of human knowledge has been recorded in books that have been saved by libraries, but increasingly it is being captured and stored on video. Certainly we know that there now seems to be video coverage of almost everything that becomes news. And often events become news simply because there is video coverage. Cell phones and PDAs that can capture small amounts of video allow us to view comedians' unrehearsed racist outbursts, gun rampages in the trenches, and silly pet antics.

Scocca (2006) makes the point that through clips of shows, sports moments, etc., not only can we see events, but we can also go back and evaluate quality. The popularity of a television show can be noted and described in a book, but the ability to view the show itself gives researchers the ability to see for themselves what all the fuss was about. Video has become an important primary source for answering questions such as these. Can talent withstand the test of time? Did a politician emphasize this word or that one, thus changing the meaning of a sentence? Just what was the size of the crowd when the camera zoomed out?

This understanding of video makes us realize the relevance of libraries being engaged in collecting video. It is a storable and retrievable medium that contains information and knowledge that can be valuable to society in new times and places. Video has been a medium that libraries have collected for some time, and it seems to only be gaining importance as a format. If collecting video is appropriate, then perhaps it is also possible to go one step further and create it as well. As libraries take a more active role in aiding content creation due to the economic crisis in scholarly communication and advances in technologies, so too can they take a more active role in creating videos.

Given the various ways in which digital stories can help libraries navigate the challenges and changes in the world of information, many types of stories will likely prove useful. We are beginning to see creative expression through video relating to library issues, to library personnel, and to examination of information shifts. There is room for much more.

Some highlights of the evolution of content-creation in video format by libraries include:

- *e-Literate* (University of California–Los Angeles, Graduate School of Education and Information Science, 2000): Perhaps one of the first attempts at providing a look at information literacy in video format came in 2000. It was distributed to

6500 schools and libraries on videotape and then streamed online when copies were exhausted. A Spanish version of this exists on *YouTube*.

- *Explore the Undergrad Library* (2007): A commercial introduction to the University of Illinois at Urbana-Champaign Undergraduate Library for incoming freshman, highlighting the various features of the library.
- *A Fair(y) Use Tale* (2007): A copyright primer told by a cast of unsuspecting Disney characters.
- *Finding Time in the Penn State Libraries* (2007): A funny look at how complicated it is to get to *Time Magazine* electronically through a library interface.
- *The L-Team* (2007): An *A-Team* parody introducing the staff of the Williams College library for Welcome Week.
- *Medieval Help Desk* (2007): An English-subtitled version of a humorous Norwegian video shows a monk learning how to operate a book much as a new computer user would struggle with that new technology.
- *Valdosta State University* (2007): A sarcastic, but educational look at the issue of plagiarism, as well as teasers for library events.
- *Web 2.0 . . . The Machine is Us/ing Us* (2007): A fast-paced look at how text is changing and becoming less fixed and more pliable, and at how the Web is changing not only information but also relationships. Created by an anthropology professor at Kansas State University.

These are but a few of the library-related videos available at the time of this writing. Certainly more are available and more will be coming. These and other videos show an insightful melding of text and video. They also provoke thought about how new technologies are challenging library tradition, text, information, and copyright. Already these videos show that libraries are prepared to learn, to build with, and share this powerful medium with which younger users are so comfortable. The videos in this list, however, are not particularly emotionally compelling. This is not to say they are not educationally useful. Some are thought-provoking. Some are just silly. But digital stories can provide a different layer of texture to the tapestry of library videos and provide a new way of involving our users in our libraries.

REFERENCES

A Fair(y) Use Tale. (2007). Retrieved June 13, 2007, from http://www.youtube.com/watch?v=CJn_jC4FNDo.

Association of College and Research Libraries. (May 16, 2007). *Information literacy standards for higher education.* Retrieved June 13, 2007, from http://www.ala.org/ala/acrl/acrlstandards/informationliteracycompetency.htm.

Brown, J. S., Denning, S., Groh, K., and Prusak, L. (2005). *Storytelling in organizations: Why storytelling is transforming 21st century organizations and management.* Boston, MA: Elsevier.

Carlson, Scott. (April 20, 2007). Are reference desks dying out? *The Chronicle of Higher Education,* 53, A37. Retrieved June 13, 2007, from http://chronicle.com.proxy.lib.ohio-state.edu/weekly/v53/i33/33a03701.htm.

Explore the Undergrad Library. (2007). Retrieved June 13, 2007, from http://tuxedo.housing.uiuc.edu/video/UGL/07UndergradLibrary.wmv.

Finding Time in the Penn State Libraries. (2007). Retrieved June 13, 2007, from http://www.youtube.com/watch?v=tKvR0OC4nYc.

Giles, James. (2005). Internet encyclopedias go head to head. *Nature,* 438, 900–901. Retrieved April 15, 2007, from http://www.nature.com/news/2005/051212/full/438900a.html.

Lambert, J. (2002). *Digital storytelling: Capturing lives, creating community.* Berkeley, CA: Digital Diner Press.

Maness, Jack M. (2006). Library 2.0 theory: Web 2.0 and its implications for libraries. *Webology,* 3. Retrieved May 1, 2007, from http://www.webology.ir/2006/v3n2/a25.html.

Medieval Help Desk. (2007). Retrieved June 13, 2007, from http://www.youtube.com/watch?v=aUczKPXWLAM.

OCLC. (March 2003). Five-year information format trends. *OCLC Membership Reports.* Retrieved June 7, 2007, from http://www.oclc.org/reports/2003format.htm.

Pink, D. H. (2005). *A whole new mind: Moving from the information age to the conceptual age.* New York: Riverhead Books.

Sax, B. (2006). Storytelling and the "information overload." *On the Horizon,* 14, 165–170.

Scocca, T. (August 31, 2006). The YouTube devolution. *The New York Observer.* Retrieved August 28, 2006, from http://www.observer.com/printpage.asp?iid=13130&ic=Off+the+Record.

Searing, S. and Lucht, K. S. (2006). The Library as place: The changing nature and enduring appeal of library buildings and spaces. *UI Current LIS Clips,* September 2006. Retrieved October 6, 2006, from http://clips.lis.uiuc.edu/2006_09P2.html.

Shapiro, J. J. and Hughes, S. K. (March/April 1996). Information literacy as a liberal art. *Educom Review,* 31. Retrieved May 1, 2007, from http://www.educause.edu/pub/er/review/reviewarticles/31231.html.

Smith, K. (2003). On specialization. In Martin Raisch (Ed.), *Musings, meanderings, and monsters, too: Essays on academic librarianship* (pp. 166–171). Lanham, MD: Scarecrow Press.

The L-Team. (2007). Retrieved June 13, 2007, from http://www.youtube.com/watch?v=YwCUtpbUWgk.

University of California–Los Angeles, Graduate School of Education and Information Science. (2003). *e-Literate: Promoting 21st century literacy skills*. Retrieved May 9, 2007, from http://www.newliteracies.gseis.ucla.edu/publications/E_literateSurveyReport.pdf.

Valdosta State University. (2007). Retrieved June 13, 2007, from http://books.valdosta.edu/media/library_films.htm.

Ward, D. (2006). Revisioning information literacy for lifelong meaning. *Journal of Academic Librarianship*, 32, 396–402.

Wesch, M. (January 31, 2007). *Web 2.0... How the Web is us/ing us*. Retrieved June 13, 2007, from http://www.youtube.com/watch?v=6gmP4nk0EOE.

Wilkinson, D. M. and Huberman, B. A. (2007). Assessing the value of cooperation in *Wikipedia*. *First Monday*, 12. Retrieved June 6, 2007, from http://firstmonday.org/issues/issue12_4/wilkinson/index.html.

Windham, C. (2006). Getting past Google: Perspectives on information literacy from the Millennial mind. *ELI Paper* 3. Retrieved May 1, 2007, from http://www.educause.edu/ir/library/pdf/ELI3007.pdf.

Winerip, Michael. (May 20, 2007). A childhood issue? Ask a librarian. *New York Times*. Retrieved May 24, 2007, from http://select.nytimes.com/search/restricted/article?res=F4061EFA3B550C738EDDAC0894DF404482.

CHAPTER 6
Campus Digital Storytelling: Partnerships and Programs

Creating a supportive environment for digital storytelling, either within the library or across the campus, has to be deliberate, collaborative and programmatic if anything meaningful is to result. It is one thing to value digital storytelling and to sponsor a workshop or two, but turning those first tentative steps into a real programmatic campus effort is quite another thing. Obstacles can get in the way, such as skepticism about the usefulness of library stories or the appropriateness of storytelling in higher education, inertia, lack of community, and competing priorities.

For the library to lead or engage in a digital storytelling program on campus, the library's administration must support that participation. Bringing in trainers, for example from the Center for Digital Storytelling (CDS), can cost several thousand dollars. Allowing librarians and staff the time they need to attend a three- or four-day workshop costs money and diverts attention from day-to-day responsibilities. If the initial workshop grows into a regular programmatic offering, participants will require additional time away from their day-to-day responsibilities. Investing in new hardware and software and hiring additional staff with multimedia expertise also costs money. Administration may not support digital storytelling wholeheartedly at first, but often initial support—perhaps for an on-campus workshop—can be won by inviting administrators to a presentation where actual digital stories are exhibited. We have found that the stories themselves make their own most powerful case. Our goal is that the administration begins to consider digital storytelling part of the staff's day-to-day responsibilities, something of real value to the institution.

A digital storytelling program needs enthusiastic storytellers and a structure with which to support them. This presents a bit of a chicken and egg dilemma, however, because the best way to create enthusiasm for such a program is to show stories made by your own community. It is also true that various units within the university may already be experimenting with aspects of digital storytelling, but may not be calling their efforts "digital stories" or, conversely, may be calling something "digital storytelling" that represents something different than what we have been discussing. For instance, the Marketing/Communications Department likely already knows the importance of stories in winning new students over to the institution. They may be featuring current students in television commercials telling personal stories of how they came to choose a major or decide on a career, but because they are not calling these commercials "digital stories" they may not realize the benefits of joining forces with the library. Academic units might be experimenting with podcasting for educational purposes and calling it "digital storytelling." Student organizations may be creating videos for fun or to document their activities. All of these efforts provide opportunities for partnerships that would both enable and strengthen the library's efforts and in turn gain further support from library administration. But we first need to figure out who is doing what.

Libraries can fill a variety of necessary roles in a campus digital storytelling program. For instance, what might originally look like an opportunity to start a program in fact may be an opportunity to bring existing programs together. If a unit outside the library is already leading an effort to bring existing programs together, there is no sense reinventing the wheel. If programs are hidden within their departments, however, the library may be able to fill the role of unifying these efforts into a single campuswide initiative. Some academic units may be using digital storytelling in classes with students, but the library might be in a position to extend the program to include faculty, staff, and graduate students from across the campus.

Another role the library can fill is to inform campus video production efforts with the meaning-making potential of storytelling. In this day of *YouTube*, a cacophony of video is being produced and shared. Garage bands are using it to share their music *MTV*-style. Activists are giving lectures. Clips from popular and professionally produced television shows are there, some with pending lawsuits. Teenagers have giggly videos lacking any sort of point, and silly stunts and spoofs abound.

This is fine for a mass media effort like *YouTube*, but is not necessarily the kind of video that will create meaningful community on campus. Bringing meaning to stories and incorporating them into the classroom, into organizational development, into campus outreach, and into supporting the institution's academic plan will move a program forward.

Yet another role that the library can fill is providing various means for sharing stories. It might mean providing copyright guidance on material that can and cannot be used to make a story available on the Web. It might mean storing videos on a streaming server with a discovery tool for finding them such as an institutional repository. It might mean saving them for posterity, just as the library traditionally has preserved so many text-based stories, but now perhaps in that institutional repository.

All this serves to illustrate that there is no single clear path to follow to make digital storytelling programmatic. A variety of steps contribute to creating a program that will ensure successful story-making, story-sharing, and community-building. The pieces needed will vary from environment to environment. Some practical ideas for where and how to begin, however, are provided here for:

- Finding storytellers
- Supporting storytellers
- Creating a storytelling community
- Assessing the program

FINDING STORYTELLERS

Stories require storytellers, and there are almost certainly many storytellers on any campus. In our own workshops we have seen an undergraduate student employee, graduate students, library and non-library staff, agricultural extension staff, librarians, and current and retired nonlibrary faculty. Digital storytelling can be conducted as an outreach program by the college or university, making the potential audience even wider. It can gather stories from alumni and can engage businesses and others in the neighborhood around the campus. Only the resources that can be made available for a storytelling program will limit the potential audience and the growth of participation.

The trick is to bring these people together into an environment where they can learn to tell their stories. There are a variety of ways to do this. Showcases are a powerful starting place in which to lead with examples. Screening stories at a showcase likely will enthuse many in the audience and will encourage people to begin to discover their own stories. The nature of these stories is such that people always feel some connection to them because they find a piece of themselves in others' stories. Then, as if involved in a conversation, they begin to believe that they too have something to contribute. If no stories have been made on your campus yet, the CDS has stories on its Web site, and an increasing number of other educational and media organizations also have stories posted on Web sites listed in the Appendix.

A showcase of digital stories should include time to introduce the concept of digital storytelling, to discuss reasons for starting a program, to discuss the sample stories, and to answer questions. Find the people who are excited by the idea of digital storytelling and who have a vision for creating such a program on your own campus to manage such a session. Include at least one person who has experience with the software used for making digital stories to answer technical questions. Use the showcase as a venue to have interested people sign up for more information and to begin forming a community of interest.

Another way to find storytellers is to schedule digital storytelling workshops and advertise these to the campus community. Unless you are specifically trying to reach a particular group on campus, this advertising should be as general as possible. Sessions with graduate students, faculty, and staff are inspiring and allow groups to form that might not ever form otherwise. A built-in incentive for a variety of interests is the promise that people can leave the workshop with a completed video they have created. Undergraduate students could also be an audience, but the reality is that undergrads are most likely to participate in digital storytelling in a classroom setting and for a grade. To involve undergraduates, it is best to start with the faculty and graduate students who can incorporate digital storytelling into their classrooms.

Yet another way to begin building a community of storytellers is to work with a department or unit with whom the library already is collaborating. Perhaps there is a way to combine their content knowledge or technical expertise with your skills and knowledge of access, copyright, and information storage. The Film, Communications, English, or other academic departments might bring skills in video, visual, and written composition required for good stories. The Music Department might provide soundtrack composition expertise. Administrative units such as the Offices of Communications, Admissions, or Information Technology might provide complementary resources and abilities.

Such partnerships not only strengthen expertise but also sow more seeds of community. They allow library staff to move outside the library by working with other campus units and in so doing gain greater understanding of the campus. By the same token those other campus units will broaden their understanding of the library's capabilities.

SUPPORTING STORYTELLERS

Because the library fills the unique role on campus of both supporting teaching and learning and actually teaching, too, the library has some unique support roles to play in the digital storytelling process. While a variety of campus units can contribute many pieces of a digital storytelling puzzle, the library is uniquely qualified to contribute others.

One likely place to begin is to offer to house digital stories on a library server. We have found that sometimes groups are working on storytelling projects already but have no way to adequately store their work. The role of "publishing" and storing the digital output of the campus community through institutional repositories is a growing role for libraries already. This role in the digital storytelling program allows the library to become part of the storytelling community by extending their traditional service of saving and providing access to information to saving and sharing the stories. The stories created in a campus digital storytelling program may or may not directly relate to a storyteller's academic work, but including personal stories in a scholarly environment enriches the sense of community. Lacking an institutional repository, the library might partner with academic computing support to run a streaming server and create a finding aid for the stories that are housed there. Finding aids should be created in such a way as to encourage classroom as well as departmental and administrative use of stories.

Copyright concerns in the digital storytelling environment center around images and music. With both so easy to find and download, it is important that images and music be used ethically and legally. If stories remain tightly held by their campus creators, copyright will not present much of a challenge, but as soon stories are moved to the Web a more sound institutional approach to following copyright guidelines is prudent. A recent study shows that college students are "universally underinformed and misinformed about the law" (Eggerton 2007, para. 4) of copyright. This applies both to their use of other people's content and their own rights as creators. Even for faculty, the brave new world of digital media and ease of sharing it challenges long held understandings of what is ethical and legal.

Therefore, another good fit for the library within a campus digital storytelling program is to offer advice on copyright issues to the storytellers. In fact, the offer to house and store stories will almost naturally lead to discussions about copyright and human subjects rules. It offers the library a chance to provide leadership on best practices for copyright compliance, to educate the campus community on these issues in regards to digital materials, and to help steer some of the storytelling process by helping people avoid copyright problems that would prevent their stories from being shared.

While the library does not usually have any particular expertise in the rules and regulations relating to research involving human subjects, it can make program participants aware of some of the implications for their stories if they involve human subjects. We learned a valuable lesson in this regard from our colleague from the College of Education and Human Ecology who created the story about his research on imaginative inquiry in the elementary classroom. While he of course had obtained parental informed consent to conduct research in the classroom and even to take still photographs of the children, he had not anticipated creating a digital story about the project to show at professional conferences. Before he could safely present his story at those conferences, he had to have all the children's nametags digitally erased from the video using PhotoShop, a time-consuming process. Without consent from all the parents to provide open access through the Web, something that would be most difficult to obtain retrospectively, he will not be able to store his story on our institutional repository.

CREATING A STORYTELLING COMMUNITY

A digital storytelling program likely will necessitate the collaboration of several units. Every organization will vary in terms of the expertise available in-house to organize and teach digital storytelling. A team that will organize and teach digital storytelling to the library or to the wider campus environment should have skills for facilitating story circles and teaching digital image, soundtrack, and video editing.

The story circle involves helping the participants find their stories. This environment needs someone who values stories, who can create a supportive and safe environment, who can ask good questions, who can develop a sense of community within the group, and who can encourage everyone to participate in each other's stories. This person might be a librarian, might be a member of technology support unit, might be faculty in the English or Communications department, a staff member of the Human Resources office, or might be a qualified graduate assistant. People from a variety of professions can have the skills necessary for running a story circle, but creative writing faculty or other people trained in facilitating group work might have stronger skills.

Digital photo editing skills are best found in a graphic designer, photographer, or academic design department faculty because these people use these skills daily. Graphic designers know the ins and outs of design software and likely will have had to work out many of the kinds of problems participants might encounter. Lambert (2002) gives specifications for such things as image size for importing photos into a digital movie, however, so the team member who will support photo editing need not figure out that piece from scratch.

A storytelling community will need access to a technology-rich facility. It is important that participants in digital storytelling have access to both software and hardware needed for the project. Software such as PhotoShop or iMovie may not be standard on institution computers and may not be available to the individuals who participate. Such participants will need access to a facility that has a fixed computer lab or a bank of properly outfitted laptops.

Server space for storing work in progress is also required. Even short three- to five-minute movies start becoming large files as more images, moving video, audio, and soundtracks are added. The final product can be saved in a reasonably sized file format, but a work in progress can require several gigabytes of file space. An alternative to server space could be an external storage drive.

Participants also need technology support outside of workshop time. This is one reason a permanent lab or multimedia production space might be a useful setting for the participants. It would allow workshop participants to know where the help is, and perhaps establish relationships with those who will be available to them outside of workshop hours. In general, workshop participants may not be able to finish every detail of what they need to do within workshop time and having access to equipment and personnel outside of that setting is important. This is one reason for including media or technology units in a digital storytelling team.

Workshops are an important part of creating a storytelling community. Besides the need to have experts available to teach them, there are a number of logistical issues to consider as well. This involves the usual issues of scheduling, coordinating, and advertising that any workshop has. There are other specific issues that also need to be worked out to best advantage.

The number of hours a storytelling workshop should encompass is about twenty to twenty-five hours. These could be done over three intensive days, four or five consecutive weekly sessions, or sessions spread out over a quarter or semester. There is no single best scenario, and the success of the schedule will depend on the participants' needs. If workshops are offered as outreach projects to noncampus participants, a more intense and shorter schedule such as a three-day session likely will support keeping the participants on track and engaged. If the workshop includes staff that cannot easily obtain three days away from the job, shorter sessions over a longer period of time might work better. Faculty who teach will need to work these sessions around their teaching schedule. If digital storytelling is a component of student course work, obviously the course schedule will dictate when meetings are held.

The size of the group and commitment of workshop participants is another consideration. Our experience has shown that it is worth having participants register for workshops. This helps set limits on the number in a group and helps participants understand the time commitment involved. It keeps the casual joiner at bay. Because of the time invested by workshop leaders, it is best to include only those who have a true interest in seeing a project through, not those who think it might be fun or interesting but who do not really have time to devote to completing a finished movie.

Limiting the number of participants per workshop to twelve or fifteen at most is useful for a variety of reasons. Giving everyone plenty of time to share their stories and get feedback in the story circle takes time, usually about fifteen minutes each. It is such an important part of the storytelling process that no one's story should receive short shrift. Another reason for keeping the numbers down is to be sure that workshop leaders can meet the support needs of participants as they begin to work with the software. Many of the participants will not be techno-savvy, and even if they are, integrating all of these applications into one digital movie may be new territory for them. Some participants will need extensive one-on-one attention and will become frustrated or disengaged if they have to wait too long for a leader to help them.

Once a workshop has concluded, it is important to acknowledge the stories that have been created. This might be done through a final screening just for the workshop participants themselves or might be done as a wider screening for others on campus or in the wider community. Such acknowledgment is important for several reasons. First, it helps to ensure that stories are actually completed. If the workshops are not part of a course curriculum where projects have to be completed for a grade, or are not part of a specific work-related project, it is easy for a story project to drift and never come to completion. Participants will be glad, no matter the reason for their involvement, to have a completed story. Workshop coordinators also need movies to show administrators and others from whom they need support for the program.

Sharing completed stories is also an important part of the story process to realize the full circle of community-building that digital stories offer. The workshop participants have heard all the other stories from the point of the germ of an idea, but it is magical for them to see a story in its fully realized state. It also helps participants build community with others in their department, or campus, or in whatever meaningful context completed stories can be shared. It helps the wider community connect with the stories, and it emboldens storytellers to continue to share their stories. Often, personal elements are hard to share, but helping participants get through sharing one story makes it more likely they will keep open the lines of communicating this story and others yet to come.

There is a final learning piece that participants take away by seeing how others also have struggled from concept to reality and what feedback from the group individuals have chosen to incorporate in their work. Depending on how these completed stories are shared, storytellers may further benefit from seeing the reactions of an even larger community. While placing stories on a Web site for worldwide distribution might eventually open broader communication, a more immediate and personal reaction from a face-to-face audience provides a unique level of closure to the storyteller. Of course, the whole point of making these stories digital is that the stories live on and continue to have an effect, but real people need real feedback too.

ASSESSING THE PROGRAM

After one full cycle of digital story creation the storytelling team will be faced with the questions of whether or not to repeat the cycle and, if so, when and how often. There are no clear-cut answers. What other time constraints do the team members have? What level of priority does digital storytelling enjoy relative to other job duties? Is there enough administrative support now to make this a regular part of participants' jobs? Is there enough demand for ongoing workshops?

As with any program, it is important to step back and assess the work the program has done, the effect it is having, and how well these efforts and their effects match library and larger institutional goals. Increasingly, library goals are being aligned more closely with the academic and strategic plans of their institutions. It is best to assess the impact of a digital storytelling program in light of such goals. While it is often tempting to look just at quantitative values in the course of such an assessment (such as numbers of stories made, numbers of workshop participants, and numbers of showcase attendees) the higher value assessment likely will be qualitative.

A qualitative approach might ask questions about how the digital storytelling program is affecting the academic and outreach missions of the university. Are faculty teaching differently by using stories? Are they engaging students in different ways, and if so, how? What motivational role have stories played in the classroom? Are faculty using stories to talk about their research? Are they engaging their colleagues around the world on a different level? How does presenting research in the context of a story change the tenor of their collegial discussions? What effect might this have or does this have on scholarly communication?

Qualitative questions might also be library-specific. What effect has the digital storytelling program had on library outreach and engagement goals? Have partnerships in digital story making led to partnerships of a different kind than the library has engaged in up until now, such as engaging with new groups for archiving projects, providing copyright expertise, or discussing new scholarly communication efforts? What kinds of stories are participants creating? Are personal stories being meaningfully incorporated in the information literacy curriculum across campus? Are storytellers learning to move the craft into their professional lives successfully? Is the library's story being told in more complex and rich ways? Such qualitative questions are more difficult to assess, but are more true to the very intent of storytelling.

OUR OWN CASE STUDY

The authors' own efforts took a path that can serve as one route to creating a program. As we described in Chapter 2, our efforts started with a journey to a workshop offered by the CDS. Our exposure to this process not only produced a story, but gave us insights into how this might benefit our own library and the university. We created our story in 2005, pre-*YouTube,* when self-produced amateur video was only beginning to be explored. We produced a library story that drew from our own experience and incorporated our own emotions and point of view.

We returned to our campus and organized a brown bag session to present our story. We invited people from our academic computing support organization, the campus humanities institute, a multimedia support group within the College of Arts and Sciences, and library staff. We were encouraged to carry on by the general excitement that greeted our presentation. We also received important support from Ohio State's Digital Union, the university's center for emerging teaching and research technology. Although we had returned from Asheville to campus inspired to bring digital storytelling to our campus, one three-day workshop experience had not given us the expertise to turn around and teach others. Therefore, our next step was to bring the CDS to campus and let others experience what we had. Joe Lambert and an assistant came and gave a three-day intensive workshop to fifteen campus participants. This group included eleven library staff, one nonlibrary faculty member, one graduate student, and two members of Ohio State's Technology Enhanced Learning and Research (TELR) unit. Lambert stayed an extra day to help us showcase the work done by this group to the university community.

As we had hoped, the showcase generated further interest in the idea of digital storytelling. We then began to organize a group of library staff to begin working on stories with support from the Digital Union. In the meantime, one of the TELR attendees began to organize a group of campus visual communicators to work on stories. Each group separately garnered plenty of interest but ultimately demonstrated little productivity largely because of a lack of a cohesive set of skills to guide ideas to completion as fully realized stories.

Eventually, the library joined forces with TELR, and coincidentally the Digital Union hired a program coordinator who also happened to be a film artist. She was able to contribute an expertise to the campus effort that we previously had lacked. After the library group joined the visual communicators group things began to happen. Out of a total of fifteen participants who came in and out of the program throughout fall quarter of 2006, five stories were produced. Concurrently, two faculty members who had participated in Joe Lambert's workshop decided to offer digital storytelling as an option for student projects in their classes, one at the graduate level, and the other at the undergraduate level. We organized and advertised a showcase for the university that drew an audience of about forty people. Five staff and faculty stories and four student stories were shown at this event.

At that fall showcase and afterward to a wider audience, we advertised a winter session and had seventeen people register from all over campus. Registrants included one faculty member from the English Department and another from the College of Veterinary Medicine, two staff from our Agricultural Extension office, a staff member from our Faculty and Teaching Assistant Development office, a graduate student, a staff photographer, a retired Social Work faculty member, a Media Center staff member, two members of our academic computing support office, a staff member from the technology support desk, a staff member from the College of Engineering and we two librarians. Out of this large group, several members needed to discontinue their involvement for a variety of reasons, but ten participants saw the workshop through to the end. Again, we organized a showcase for the campus and were able to showcase the ten stories completed by our group. (The English Department faculty member subsequently developed an undergraduate course in media composition the culminating project for which was production of a digital story by every member of the class.)

We now have begun to collect some of the stories that were created in our workshops into our institutional repository. Not all participants are comfortable with sharing their stories on the Web, and not all can because of copyright restrictions on music or images they have used. We hope that when we obtain a critical mass of stories in the repository others will be inspired to add their stories, and a virtual community will begin to form. Our institutional repository does not yet offer the feedback options available on *YouTube*, but it does provide an opportunity to brand these as the stories of our institution. They also are searchable and discoverable through *Google*. Some digital stories newly created as video podcasts soon will be available through iTunesU.

Shortly after our last formal workshop some campus administrators asked us to step back to assess the program. Everyone, including us, has realized that this is a highly labor intensive program, and the benefits may not be obvious to those who have not participated in the storytelling circles. Yet even though initial quantitative assessment efforts indicated that the benefits might not be obvious, those benefits might be greater and more complex than originally anticipated. While our assessment is not fully realized at this writing, our initial discussions with participants at all levels lead us to believe we will uncover unanticipated positive outcomes.

For example, the faculty member who created the story about his research has indicated that he encounters different types of discussions at conferences when he includes his digital story in his presentations. As we described in Chapter 4, another faculty member has used digital storytelling in her biology class. One faculty member is using her new video skills to make a movie for an outreach program aimed at interesting middle-school-aged girls in veterinary medicine as a career.

A librarian who created a digital story indicates that the process completely influenced the development of a student-mentoring program she was designing for the library. The students hired for this mentoring program, Peer Library Tutors, for two years produced stories about how working in the library promoted their intellectual and personal development. We are examining ways of showcasing these for a further ripple effect. An orientation game being developed by our library's Instruction Office incorporates a digital story made by a library staff member about one of our special collections. That same story will be featured on the Web-based finding aid for that particular collection. A story created by a Preservation Office student assistant has enhanced the training program the library gives to new student employees. It is not a "how to" video but a "why" video that increases understanding of the overall mission and values of the library.

Some of these implications are hard to track and have required lots of conversations and pure happenstance to unearth. We do need to unearth these outcomes, however, and discover what further effects they are having on the academic mission of the institution. We think that by articulating these effects more broadly and precisely others will be as interested in this medium as we are.

REFERENCES

Eggerton, J. (April 10, 2007). Study: Students don't understand copyright rules. *Broadcasting and Cable*. Retrieved April 26, 2007, from http://www.broadcastingcable.com/article/CA6432259.html.

Lambert, J. (2002). *Digital storytelling: Capturing lives, creating community*. Berkeley, CA: Digital Diner Press.

CHAPTER 7
Realizing Community

We began this book by looking at the ways in which human beings use their apparently innate urge to tell stories to create both their individual identities and their social identities. We also noted that until now storytelling may not have been considered a legitimate enterprise for academic libraries, whether those reasons lie in a perceived lack of seriousness or scientific objectivity. We hope that we have demonstrated many of the reasons to support digital storytelling efforts in academic libraries and, more specifically, to tell library stories. Understanding the educational and social value of stories provides both a context and rationale for storytelling, but there are additional reasons why libraries should value a program of digital storytelling, the most important being the potential of digital stories to foster community within the library and across the campus.

Stories can help the library navigate its way through the chaotic changes assaulting the library world and higher education in general (Sax 2006). Stories can help the library appreciate its own strengths as it negotiates new roles and new identities. Stories can help change our users' expectations of us, expanding their notions of the library's usefulness and reminding them of hidden or understated benefits the library always has provided.

Library stories can be useful development tools. As the library seeks funds for renovation or other special projects, a tool with powerful emotional appeal can be the tipping point in convincing the community to contribute financial and other support. Stories from alumni can help build this constituency.

Library stories can facilitate internal organizational development. Especially in large research libraries, it is too easy to lose track of the breadth and depth of expertise that our staffs bring to our organizations. Internal strife occurs when one unit lacks understanding of why another unit is receiving a particular kind of support. Meetings in which administrators explain PowerPoint budget presentations simply cannot convey the complete message that a presentation complemented by digital stories about the employees in various library units can.

UTOPIA?

So far, we know of no completely perfect programs of digital storytelling in academic libraries, including our own. Even if ours were a perfect program, it probably would not meet the needs of another institution. Here we offer, however, a utopian view of what a perfect program might look like.

In our utopia, the digital storytelling program would operate out of the library's Outreach Department, a department whose other responsibilities might include internal and external communications, training, grant-seeking and administration, and campus and community outreach. A librarian assisted by an administrative manager would chair this department. Among the chair's responsibilities would be motivating the library's digital storytelling program. The administrative manager, his staff and student assistants would ensure the program's smooth day-to-day functioning. A digital storytelling advisory committee with a new chair appointed every three years by the Outreach Department would consist of librarians, library staff, and faculty and staff from around the campus. Frequently rotating leadership and membership would ensure new ideas and fresh supplies of energy. The Outreach Department would hire and train a cadre of student assistants who would be available to team with librarians who had the content for digital stories but who lacked the time or technological skills to produce fully finished stories.

The program would ensure that workshops were held regularly and that they met the scheduling needs of librarians, staff, and student assistants. Nonlibrary faculty, staff, and student assistants would be included. Some workshops would be limited to librarians or classroom faculty, others to staff, others to student assistants or students not employed by the library. Some librarians and faculty would appreciate having their own librarianship and teaching needs met in an environment that does not expose their lack of expertise to staff and student eyes. Staff would appreciate the freedom of expression they often lack in their work environment. Students would appreciate the noncensorious environment of working with a group of other students with no faculty or possible supervisors around. On the other hand, some workshops would be open to all of the campus or the local community, regardless of status.

The format of the workshops would vary, depending on the time of year. During the regular (non-summer) academic year, workshops would be spread out in sessions over a series of weeks or months. The size of these groups would be limited to twelve participants because, even with this size group, story circles take about three hours; and inexperienced creators need considerable help in the technical sessions. Once time constraints catch up with people over the course of a quarter or semester, the group of twelve often decreases to a more ideal group size of eight. We would not start with a smaller group—for instance, eight—because if three or four participants dropped out we would be left with what we considered to be less than a critical mass.

In the first workshop session, required only of newcomers, workshop leaders would review the concept of digital storytelling and Lambert's (2002) seven elements, and they would show samples of digital stories to get participants' creative juices flowing. Leaders and participants would critique the sample stories in terms of the seven elements. Leaders also would preview for participants the kinds of images or videos they should be collecting in anticipation of the session on image scanning and manipulation with PhotoShop or other image-editing software. Participants would learn about campus resources for borrowing digital cameras and digital video cameras, as well as copyright-free video and audio resources on the Web.

Newcomers and experienced digital storytellers all would return for the second session of the workshop, the story circle, about two weeks later, prepared with at least a rough script. Everyone would read their scripts and receive feedback on their stories from the rest of the story circle. They would enjoy reacting to the stories others have to tell. Two weeks later we would hold a session on PhotoShop; two weeks after that a session on iMovie (or Movie Maker or Adobe Premier); and two weeks after that a session on GarageBand, including actually recording voiceover narratives. Having built their basic digital story, participants would use the rest of the sessions—perhaps two or three—for fine-tuning their movies, including creating and importing a soundtrack and preparing for showcasing their stories first to the other workshop participants and then to the campus community.

This extended workshop format would allow a wide variety of people to participate without having to sacrifice a full, continuous four days. Faculty could teach their classes, staff could get their work done, and student assistants and other students could work and attend their classes. In the summer, however, the Outreach Department would offer one or two intensive, continuous four-day workshops for no more than eight participants each. The schedule would look like this:

- Morning 1: Introduction/review, plus the seven elements; story circle
- Afternoon 1: Scanning and PhotoShop
- Morning 2: Importing and working with images/video in iMovie
- Afternoon 2: Recording voiceovers in GarageBand and importing into iMovie
- Morning 3: Creating soundtrack and importing into iMovie
- Afternoon 3: Syncing video with audio tracks; transitions and titles
- Morning 4: Fine-tuning; compressing files and preparing for showcases
- Afternoon 4: Workshop showcase

On Day 5, the campus community showcase would be held with participants each introducing their story. Because this schedule is ambitious, staff and lab space would be available in the evenings to help participants. The Outreach Department would sponsor a social get-together for participants after Afternoon 1 and after the workshop showcase on Afternoon 4. It also would provide enticing refreshments for the campus showcases.

A wealth of stories would result from our workshops. A special collections librarian would tell a series of stories all of which revolved around a single manuscript in the rare books and manuscripts collection. One story would tell about the manuscript itself, its author, how it came to be written, and the "story within a story" told by the author's marginal notes. Another would focus on the donor. Who was this person, what fascinated him about this area of collecting, and why did he give or sell this manuscript to the library? The third would feature an interview with a scholar who had studied the manuscript to bring to life the importance of this document to a scholar's life. The catalog record for this manuscript would link to these stories so scholars and students from all over the world could access the personal stories relating to the document. The stories might even be used in recruiting new faculty.

A group of library staff members might tell stories about how they have dealt with changes in how they do their jobs over the decades they have worked in the library. Or, they might respond to changes in the library's organization. They might tell stories about the sheer volume of work they have accomplished for the library, about the street people they have dealt with, or about a colleague who is about to retire.

Word would spread around the campus that the workshops were fun and that the technical skills they taught would be useful for students' work in an increasing variety of classes. Student assistants would vie for places in the workshops and recommend their friends too for participation. The students—fortified by utopian quantities of refreshments, of course—would create stories about their personal lives, their communities, and their friends. With guidance from workshop leaders, many of whom would be librarians and classroom faculty, they would move on to creating stories about the people they worked with in the library and about memorable faculty. Most importantly, they would begin to use the digital story format to reflect on what they were learning in class.

For example, in an English class a student might have been reading some American ghost stories written by women. In her History class she might have been studying late nineteenth-century images of women in America. How have those images of women persisted into the twenty-first century, she might wonder. If I were going to tell a twenty-first-century ghost story, how might it begin? Therein would lie the germ of her digital story. Through the creative process of scripting her story and putting it together with image and sound, she would be using digital storytelling to reflect on how images of women have changed over the past centuries and how those images inform her own identity as a twenty-first-century woman.

Small communities would form with each succeeding workshop. In the story circles people would begin their first tentative steps toward learning about each other and trusting one another. As they stumbled together through learning how to use the multimedia applications and helped each other overcome minor technological disasters ("My images are all starting to zoom!"), the bonds would grow. Maybe they would share a few laughs and a few tears during the showcases. As participants moved on to future workshops, they would meet new people and new bonds would form, creating new nodes in an ever-expanding campus network of a digital storytelling community of practice. The campus digital storytelling wiki would allow people to share tips and techniques and add to a frequently asked question collection. Regular lunchtime brown-bag meetings would feature vendors who wanted to display cutting-edge technologies for use in digital storytelling.

As the quantity of stories grew, the library's Outreach Department would create routines for adding metadata, for streaming the videos in a variety of formats, and for loading the stories into campus and consortial institutional repositories. This department also would arrange with the stories' authors for appropriate *Creative Commons* licensing. Now anyone on campus, or around the world, could access the collection by author, title, subject, or other metadata tags.

None of this could be accomplished without cross-campus partnerships, and in our digital storytelling utopia the library would have formed many productive ones. We would have partnered with our own information technology staff to make sure that we had the software and hardware we needed as well as the day-to-day support to keep it up and running. This would be especially important when we were running tightly scheduled four-day workshops. How would we have cultivated this relationship with a group whose own resources of time and staff are frequently overtaxed? We would have worked with their supervisor and convinced him of the benefits of having them participate in one of our earliest workshops. In this workshop they would be able to demonstrate the sometimes advanced skills with multimedia applications that they had developed outside the workplace, they would be able to see the kinds of behind-the-scenes support we would need for the digital storytelling program, and they would be able to enjoy leading the formation of the campus digital storytelling community from its very beginning.

We also would have formed strong partnerships with the various other multimedia technology support units outside of the library, for instance the New and Emerging Technologies unit, the people on whom we depended for instruction in multimedia technologies when we first began our digital storytelling program. They also had provided the labs that we had used for our workshops until the library's own multimedia lab space was up and running. Now that the program was running smoothly, we would frequently team-teach the workshops. At least one member of this unit would serve as an *ex officio* member of the library's Outreach Department advisory committee that would be planning for future roles for technology in the library's many outreach programs to the campus and beyond, including digital storytelling.

We would have worked with the campus Legal Affairs Office to produce clear guidelines, written for the layperson, for use of multimedia images and sound in digital stories. The library's Interlibrary Services Department would have been working to create a copyright clearance procedure for use when campus community members wanted to use copyrighted images and sound files. (Remember, this would be a utopia.)

Beyond partnerships with campus information technology-related units we would have formed relationships with academic departments and academic support units such as the English Department, the History Department, the Chemistry and Design Departments. We also would have teamed with the campus Faculty Teaching Advancement Office.

For instance, our English Department teaches a course called "The Many Faces of Composition: Text, Image, and Sound." The building block assignments of the course culminate in a capstone digital story that brings together a written script, images, and soundtrack. Following an introduction by the library's copyright expert to the concept of fair use, public domain, and copyright early in the semester, librarians would have helped students identify sources of images and sound files that they could use on a fair use basis for their stories. The library would have displayed the completed stories on a flat-panel television in the library coffee shop, and taken care of preserving the stories in the campus institutional repository.

A freshman seminar offered by the History Department would involve having students bring an artifact that represents something about their family history, perhaps an old family recipe or a piece of jewelry, or a photograph of their grandfather in a military uniform. The instructor had intended to have her students research the periods and the topics represented by their artifacts and write a paper reflecting the results of that research. After she attended a digital storytelling showcase, however, she participated in a workshop to explore the instructional possibilities of digital storytelling. She then decided that she would rather have the students create digital stories that not only incorporated their historical learning but expressed their personal connection to the artifacts in a new way. Librarians not only would have worked with the class on copyright issues, finding digital video and sound files, and on preserving the stories in the institutional repository, but they would have worked with students on doing primary and secondary historical research with much more meaningful results for the students than they typically would have enjoyed without the additional engagement with multimedia composition. The faculty member would have led the story circles for her class—it would have taken two sessions—and the New and Emerging Technologies Office would have led the technology sessions. Librarians would have participated in the story circles and technology sessions so they could be informed of the students' needs and so they could provide extra pairs of hands as needed.

And the Chemistry Department? It would have selected a small group of accomplished undergraduate students and offered them a summer fellowship to work on a pilot project to produce digital stories to bring to life key concepts in the department-created electronic textbook. These students would have teamed with students from the Design Department. Librarians would have helped with the copyright, access, and preservation tasks that by now would be becoming routine, but those experienced in facilitating story circles also would have worked in tandem with chemistry faculty to help students find the "dramatic question" and the "heart" of the stories they were telling.

The library's Outreach Department would provide many other services in support of our utopian digital storytelling program, particularly marketing the program and its results to the rest of the campus community. They would publicize our campus showcases in campus listservs, student newspapers, and even would have student assistants stand in front of the library on showcase days and distribute handbills advertising the stories (and the free food). They would make sure that the university's president, provost, and other administrators—along with, of course, the library administration—were invited to attend. Announcements would include links to the campus institutional repository for access to previous stories. They also could create an online "Digital Storytelling Newsletter," linked from the library Web site that would highlight new stories, interviews with participants, and information about upcoming workshops.

The Outreach Department would manage the content of the flat-panel screens around the library and would loop digital stories along with notices of other library activities. They also would serve as eyes and ears for the Digital Storytelling Advisory Committee. When they learned that the Rare Books and Manuscripts Department was planning an exhibit on its collection of Robert Frost first editions, they would inform the chair of the Digital Storytelling Advisory Committee who would approach the Rare Books librarian about the possibility of working with one of the Outreach Department's digital storytelling students to create a story in support of the exhibit. As visitors approached a display case containing a Frost first edition they then would view a story about Frost's writing process.

The Outreach Department also would help identify and apply for grants to support our program. These grants would pay for us to bring instructors from the Center for Digital Storytelling to our campus to give key campus players some hands-on experience with creating digital stories. We even would be able to have our Provost and our Dean of Humanities sit in on a story circle. Soon, they would be looking for time in their schedules to participate in a full four-day workshop. Grants would support campus leaders' travel to national workshops sponsored by Stories for Change, as well as the Chemistry/Design student summer fellowships.

Finally, the library's Outreach Department would lead the way in finding ways to extend our digital storytelling program into the community beyond the campus. In collaboration with the campus Service Learning Office and the university's School of Education, the library would plan an after-school digital storytelling program at our neighborhood middle school. Our local district has had to sacrifice school library media specialists in the middle schools, so we would use the digital storytelling initiative as a vehicle for helping participating students become information literate. We would help them talk about the stories they want to tell and—as we did with the history assignment—about how to define the information they would need in order to learn more about the subjects of their stories, for instance, gangs or single-parent families. Fortunately, the students we work with already have free access to a number of online resources through both school and public libraries so we would show them how to use those resources to access information, then how to evaluate it and think about how they might incorporate what they have learned into their stories. We also would devote some attention to issues regarding the legal and ethical use of the information they would find, including video and sound files. The truly exciting results we anticipate, though, would be those made visible in the completed stories and in the bonds of community that would have grown among the students and between the students and ourselves.

The Outreach Department would be a branch of the library administration, and support from the very highest levels of the library administration would be crucial to our success. We would be lucky to have a Library Director who would have attended our very first presentation about digital storytelling and who would have seen the potential that this kind of initiative held for the library, for the campus community at large, and for the library's partnerships with the campus community. The library administration would provide us the time we would need to plan and lead workshops; to meet with faculty, staff, and administrators around campus; to troubleshoot processes with the Outreach Department; and to develop relationships in the off-campus community. The administration also would encourage librarians and staff to participate in the workshops themselves and to allow the staff they supervise to participate. They would provide small bonuses and other rewards for librarians and staff whose digital stories drew noteworthy attention to the library. The administration would provide the considerable amount of money that it would take to run the program, money for software and hardware, technical support, staffing, publicity, and more. In our utopia, the administration would consider digital storytelling to be an investment worth that expense.

CONCLUSION

This utopian vision has come partly true on our campus, but we have a long way to go in other respects. We have established an effective partnership with our campus Technology Enhanced Learning and Research unit which has provided much of the technological support and instruction for our workshops. Through our showcases we have interested an increasing number of faculty and staff from an increasingly wide variety of departments and support units across campus. They are creating their own stories and using digital storytelling as an instructional strategy. Others have expressed interest. The most basic challenge we always run up against is time—time to attend workshops, time to gather images and create soundtracks, time for staff to assist the increasing number of students being assigned digital storytelling projects. Nevertheless, we gradually are overcoming challenges related to staffing, scheduling, copyright, and preservation. We remain firmly convinced that digital storytelling has a place in academic libraries and that it can lead the academic library forward from the old, somewhat empty moniker of "the heart of the university" to a new more dynamic role as the "crossroads of the university" where librarians, faculty, students, and staff meet, share, and truly get to know and appreciate one another.

Library stories are worth telling for a variety of reasons. We can use stories to grow our organization and to reach out to and to listen to our users. We can use stories to create new campus collaborations and to transform those collaborations we already enjoy, further embedding ourselves in the curriculum. Just as participating in a story circle transforms both the tale and the teller, collaborating on digital storytelling within the library and across campus can transform our stories, our listeners, and in the process foster community.

Libraries should accept the fact that society is learning to receive and impart much of its information visually and that visual literacy is receiving increasing attention at all academic levels and across virtually all disciplines. Video allows for expression that text does not, yet at the same time text still allows for expression that video does not. We believe that creating digital stories can lead students back to text in the classroom and that watching others' digital stories can lead students back to our libraries' collections of written literature, history, and other representations of knowledge. Once enticed back to the library, students will be more likely to incorporate those stories into their own new knowledge and, possibly, new knowledge they are creating for the world.

In one of his commentaries on libraries and museums as cultural institutions, Carr recognizes that "in cultural institutions, moments of redefining and reorganizing our ideas, and of breaking through and transforming our images of ourselves, are immanent in all things. Though they are situations for learning in the public frame, cultural institutions induce private moments for reflecting, revising, and reinterpreting the invisible and often ambiguous texts that over time compose one life" (Carr 1991, 7). When librarians and library staff, faculty, and staff use libraries as resources for creating digital stories, libraries increase their power to become sites for just such "reflecting, revising, and reinterpreting." We have only just begun to visualize that potential, but we can see it lying just in reach on the horizon as we foster community by telling stories about ourselves.

REFERENCES

Carr, D. (1991). Minds in museums and libraries: The cognitive management of cultural institutions. *Teachers College Record*, 93, 6–27.
Lambert, J. (2002). *Digital storytelling: Capturing lives, creating community*. Berkeley, CA: Digital Diner Press.
Sax, B. (2006). Storytelling in a liminal time [electronic version]. *On the Horizon*, 14, 147–151.

Appendix: Selected List of Web Sites for Digital Storytelling

Adobe Youth Voices: http://www.adobe.com/aboutadobe/philanthropy/youthvoices/

Bay Area VideoCorporation/YouthLINK: http://www.bavc.org/nextgen/youthlink/index.html

Bridges to Understanding: http://www.bridgesweb.org/

British Broadcasting Corporation, "Capture Wales": http://www.bbc.co.uk/wales/capturewales/

Center for Digital Storytelling: http://www.storycenter.org

Digital Stories at UMBC: http://umbc.edu/oit/newmedia/studio/digitalstories/

Dr. Helen Barrett's Electronic Portfolios: http://electronicportfolios.com/

Eduweave: http://www.eduweave.org/

Home Depot True Stories: http://www6.homedepot.com/truestories/

I-10Witness Project: http://i10witness.org/

Librareo: http://www.gale.com/librareo/

National Public Radio Story Corps: http://www.storycorps.net/

National Public Radio Story Corps/Griot Initiative: http://www.storycorps.net/griot/

Ohio State University Knowledge Bank: http://kb.osu.edu

PhotoBus: http://www.photobus.co.uk

Silence Speaks: http://www.silencespeaks.org/

Stories for Change: http://storiesforchange.net/about_stories_for_change

Storybuilders: http://www.storybuilders.org/

StoryMapping Stories: http://www.storymapping.org/

Street Stories (UC–Berkeley): http://www2.sims.berkeley.edu/research/projects/socialtech

Stumble Video: http://video.stumbleupon.com/

Tech Head Stories: http://tech-head.com/dstory.htm

University of Houston, Educational Uses of Digital Storytelling: http://www.coe.uh.edu/digital-storytelling/

University of Maryland (Baltimore Campus) New Media Center Digital Stories: http://umbc.edu/oit/newmedia/studio/digitalstories/

Web 2.0 Meets Information Fluency: http://informationfluency.wikispaces.com/

YouTube: http://www.youtube.com

Index

About the Authors

ANNE M. FIELDS is Subject Specialist for English at the Ohio State University Libraries, Columbus; previous positions at Ohio State University include Coordinator for Research and Reference and Subject Specialist for Education.

KAREN R. DIAZ is an Instruction Librarian at the Ohio State University Libraries, Columbus; previous positions include Web librarian, reference librarian, and online coordinator. She also coauthored, with Nancy O'Hanlon, *IssueWeb: A Guide and Sourcebook for Researching Controversial Issues on the Web.*